AMERICA'S THIRTY YEARS WAR

WHO IS WINNING?

BALINT VAZSONYI

REGNERY PUBLISHING, INC.
Washington, D.C.

Library of Congress Cataloging-in-Publication Data

Vazsonyi, Balint.
  America's thirty years war: who is winning? / Balint Vazsonyi.
     p. cm.
  Includes index.
  ISBN 0-89526-354-8
  1. National characteristics, American. 2. United States--Politics and government--Philosophy. 3. United States--Social conditions--1980-   4. Vazsonyi, Balint. I. Title
E169.1.V39   1998
973091--dc21   98-18905
                                          CIP

Published in the United States by
Regnery Publishing, Inc.
An Eagle Publishing Company
One Massachusetts Avenue, NW
Washington, DC 20001

Distributed to the trade by
National Book Network
4720-A Boston Way
Lanham, MD 20706

Printed on acid-free paper.
Manufactured in the United States of America

10 9 8 7 6 5

Books are available in quantity for promotional or premium use. Write to Director of Special Sales, Regnery Publishing, Inc., One Massachusetts Avenue, NW Washington, DC 20001, for information on discounts and terms or call (202) 216-0600.

AMERICA'S THIRTY
YEARS WAR

Whether the United States survives as the beacon it has been will depend on the willingness of Americans to contemplate anew the reasons for its success, and to make decisions accordingly.

CONTENTS

PROPERTY

IDENTITY

IN CLOSING

ACKNOWLEDGMENTS

DR. DANIEL MCDONALD and the Potomac Foundation created the situation in which serious contemplation of the ideas, and undisturbed preparation of the text, could occur.

Beverly Danielson, Nicholas Vazsonyi, and Frank Cooper read various drafts with a critical eye, Richard Vigilante and Erica Rogers made excellent suggestions, and, finally, Patricia Bozell applied the necessary pair of benevolent scissors.

Ann Drexel, Frank Gardner, and the Intercollegiate Studies Institute expressed their faith in the form of substantial advance orders.

But there is always one person who, more than any other, becomes an indispensable participant of such a process. In this case, it has been my wife Barbara. She was the first person I met in my new home, America. She waited patiently until I began to discover America. She listened for decades to my bewildering, nearly incomprehensible political commentaries, and when I thought I was ready to speak about them in public, she absorbed all the frustrations attendant to early attempts. Naturally, she read every version of this manuscript and continued to act as a bridge between the ideas and their potential recipients.

This page would not be complete without expressing my gratitude to thousands of other Americans who, in thousands of encounters, taught me everything I know about this wondrous land.

MOTIFS

CHAPTER ONE

"THE WAY WE WERE..."

MY FIRST HAIRCUT in America should have taken place on a Wednesday in February of 1959. It didn't. There were two men talking inside the little barber shop in Tallahassee, Florida, and one of them swung around as I entered. "It's Wednesday. We're closed, sonny boy," he grunted. I left, deeply hurt. You see, although not yet twenty-three, I had already been appearing in public for ten years as a concert pianist. I was not anyone's "sonny boy."

Some months later, I needed a travel document. An immigrant's green card did not correspond to the Europeans' idea of a passport, so the good folks in Tallahassee arranged a meeting with the district's congressman, and to Washington I went. The office door, once I found it, proclaimed the Honorable Bob Sykes. "Bob?" I said to myself—"A mere youth in the hallowed halls of Congress?"

Once inside, a venerable man in his sixties rose from behind the desk. "Hi, I'm Bob," he said, stretching out a hand. That's how I learned that it was all right for me to be "sonny boy" in America.

I was a good many years away from becoming a citizen who could vote, but it didn't matter. I hardly spoke enough English to explain my quandary, a highly unusual one at that. It didn't matter. In a few minutes, "Bob" was on the phone to the Immigration and Naturalization Service and, together, these two American public servants figured out how this Hungarian refugee could have a piece of paper upon which a pedantic Swiss consular official could imprint a visa.

The year 1959 seems a century away. Having escaped from Hungary after the revolt against Soviet occupation had failed, I arrived in the United States on the 8th of January at the end of a two-day journey, the last twenty-two hours of which were spent aboard a Pan American DC-6 chartered for Hungarian refugees. We landed in New York where, after a sparse lunch, I was pushed onto a train. It took another twenty-four hours to get to Tallahassee.

Dinnertime on the train. The conductor hands me a card. The only words on the card I could understand were "check one." I had heard that America was so rich, people didn't pay with currency, they just wrote checks. I didn't have a checkbook; consequently, I assumed that I could not have dinner on the train. In any case, the $23 which represented my total earthly holdings were for an emergency.

The next day I began to "learn" America.

For sure it was strange. The people, the clothes, the houses all looked strange. As for food, I figured the quality of meat might make up for the absence of flavor; salad was obviously a religion. What? Only one kind of mustard? And why does everyone insist on making each bite difficult by putting down the knife and changing the fork over to the right hand? No one spoke any language other than English. Boys I didn't know told me to "take it easy"; girls practiced throwing batons in the air while carrying on a conversation. It was all very, very strange.

Slowly I learned to eat the food, to speak and understand the language, to live with the strange customs. Soon, I resumed my concert career, which required trips to Europe. Every time I returned, I found America a little less strange. Then, one day, the immigration officer at New York's Idlewild airport—as it was then called— admitted me with the words, "Good afternoon, sir. Welcome home."

He didn't have to say it. Remember, I wasn't even a citizen.

It was as if someone had turned on huge spotlights in my brain. For the first time, I began to contemplate the practical implications of what is called equality in the affairs of man. This much-abused phrase suddenly rang true. I knew it was the law in America, but this officer demonstrated something beyond the law. As a public servant, he was, of course, carrying out the law in examining my documents. But as a human being, he was offering me a partnership in being American. He did so without any high-minded or high-handed platitudes. He simply indicated, if I wanted to share the land he called home, that would be just fine. How much more equal can you be?

I began to look around me with different, clearer eyes. At first, I recalled, I thought it ridiculous that "real" Americans could not identify themselves. Identity papers are staples on the Continent of Europe, ranging from the "looser" Western version to the obsession that Russians—Russians, not necessarily Soviets—have with documents. Now, I realized how much that had to do with personal freedom. In Europe, West and East, you have to register your address with the police. Americans have a hard time believing this. In 1959 no American had even heard of a driver's license with a photo. And this was the only country where no one checked your papers upon departure.

Hand-in-hand with these liberties went the custom of not building fences around one's property, of not locking cars and homes, of making deals—large and small—on a handshake. Trust was in the air. People, for the most part, behaved toward one another in a civilized manner—the same way they groomed and clothed themselves. It was an entirely American phenomenon to travel on a crowded bus in summer heat, yet experience no discomfort when inhaling air through one's nostrils, unavoidable in most other countries. Appropriate conduct was expected and offered; it was also reciprocated without fail.

But the most telling difference was in attitudes. While people elsewhere operated on the premise, "If I haven't got it, he shouldn't have it either," Americans seemed to say, "If he's got it, I ought to be able to have it too, if I just work hard enough." The ability of generation after generation actually to fulfill such desires helped maintain what appeared to be a union not merely of fifty states but, more importantly, of some 250 million individuals.

By the time I got my citizenship in 1964, I was grateful and immensely proud to be told by the judge in Grand Rapids, Michigan, that I would not be a Hungarian-American, nor any other hyphenated American. While no one suggested then, or has since, that I disown or forget my upbringing, I was now, simply and officially, American.

More than three decades have passed. Are the people who come here still grateful for the opportunity? Are we still a union of some 250 million individuals? Am I still "American," plain and simple? Above all, do we still live by the principle of looking upon things others possess not with envy, but as an incentive for us to work that much harder?

Some changes are obvious. Pan American Airways is no more. On the other hand there is a profusion of mustards in every supermarket—indeed, new flavors come our way from an endless parade of chefs on television. But in the early 1960s most Americans did not build walled-in communities with guard houses. Americans knew how to live and work *together*, and new efforts were under way to make sure that this greatest of benefits would extend to all men, women, and children in the land.

That is not what happened. As we approach the end of the millennium, Americans seem to be less and less able to live and work together. We have left the path that rendered this nation unique, and uniquely successful.

CHAPTER TWO

PEDIGREE

MY FIRST ENCOUNTER with socialism occurred at the age of eight. In 1944, on a Sunday before dawn, the armed forces of the Third Reich occupied Hungary. The Third Reich was ruled by the National Socialist German Workers' Party; thus, "my first socialism" happened to be national socialism. Within days, the nazis interned or executed the leadership of all other political organizations. The world was at war, and it was not possible for an eight-year-old to distinguish between aspects of the horror: how much of it was the war, and how much of it was national socialism.

The war over, several old and new political parties competed for votes. (Prior to the German occupation, Hungary had already achieved universal suffrage, introduced by my granduncle Vilmos Vázsonyi, the last minister of justice of the Austro-Hungarian Monarchy, who also founded the National Democratic Party of Hungary.) Because the aggressive pursuit of influence by the—relatively small—Communist Party of Hungary was inescapable, I decided to read the *Communist Manifesto* by Karl Marx and Friedrich Engels. By pure chance, this happened soon after seeing *Mr. Smith Goes to Washington* with James Stewart. In retrospect, it is easy to see why reading Marx right after experiencing Jimmy Stewart should be exceptionally shocking. But even in the cool light of day, Marx radiates a degree of anger, aggression, and sheer ugliness of mind that would make acceptance of his thought difficult, were the thought persuasive.

For this reader, it was not.

By 1948, the Communist Party had assumed police authority over all economic activity, and began to classify people's political attitudes. Communist operatives worked out of the same building occupied not long before by the Gestapo and wore the same shining leather jackets as the nazis. The next year, in 1949, the communists seized complete control of the country, and declared Hungary's unconditional allegiance to the Union of Soviet Socialist Republics. As the nazis before, they interned or executed the leadership of all other political organizations.

Once again, we were controlled by the armed forces of a socialist country. This time, the world was not at war. Hungary was occupied by armored divisions of the Soviet Union to make it a part of the Russian Empire, using socialism as a pretext. In retrospect, it began to dawn on me then that, a few years back, the objective was to make Hungary a part of the Third Reich, using (national) socialism as the pretext.

Reading Marx, it seemed that socialism could be used as a pretext for just about anything—for the confiscation of people's belongings, for determining what could and could not be taught in the schools, for pronouncing what did or did not happen—and what should have happened—in the course of history. Since Marx listed more than a half dozen different kinds of socialism back in 1848, it also seemed that socialism was whatever a person said it was, and that all versions of socialism were objectionable, except the version of the person who happened to be writing—in this case, Marx. It further transpired that the ultimate goal of socialists was to build communism. That was why "real" socialists called themselves "communists." In communism, the state would assign everyone a role in the national production. There would be no place for a concert pianist as such, but, after the requisite hours in the factory, I could spend my free time playing ping-pong or the piano to my heart's content. Such absurd provisions wiped away any initial benefit of the doubt about the nature of Communism.

The year following the assumption of total control by the Communist Party, I made a comment to a fellow student, also a serious pianist. "A real artist," I said, "cannot be a communist." I was thirteen years old, and so was he. He reported my comment to the authorities. I was tried by a panel of politically correct students and given a warning. From that moment on, I was watched by the head of the students' organization who made it clear that I would remain constantly under suspicion.

By this time, my older brother was in prison. Determined to locate our father who had been missing since being carted off in one of the nazi roundups, my brother tried to get to Austria through Czechoslovakia—naturally on foot, and without a permit from the Hungarian and Soviet authorities. (The western borders had already been mined.) He was captured by Czechoslovakian police who, after taking all his possessions in exchange for a promise to let him go, promptly turned him over to the Hungarian authorities. In a mock trial, he was sentenced to eight months' imprisonment—the going rate for those between eighteen and twenty years of age who tried to cross the border.

I vowed then to leave Hungary, should the opportunity ever arise. The outlook was not good. Communist rule seemed assured as long as the Russian occupation continued, and no one harbored realistic hopes about their leaving voluntarily. It was widely understood that, at the Yalta conference, Franklin Delano Roosevelt had ceded Hungary to the USSR.

Four years later, when I was seventeen, I had the "pleasure" of another disciplinary trial. After the head of the piano department at the famed Liszt Academy gave his "communist word of honor" in public that no harm would come from a frank airing of complaints, I spoke at some length about being denied permission to go abroad either to study, or to participate in international competitions—both indispensable for budding musicians with a serious career in mind. This time, my trial involved the entire Communist Party organization of the Music Academy, the faculty, and the students. I was given to understand that the punishment would be expulsion from all institutes of higher learning.

Owing to the heroic effort of some of my professors, I got off with a stern final warning and was forbidden to give concerts for six months. Compared with some who were exiled for two years for the simple act of telling a joke about political leaders, the punishment was mild. But all my experiences confirmed the perception that socialism in all its forms placed unlimited power in the hands of persons who were contemptuous of other humans, and whose basest instincts were unleashed in the process.

Still, amidst all the gloom, the spring of 1956 brought some fresh breezes and, in October of that year, Hungary erupted in violence. For a few days, it seemed the country would be free—there would be no need to leave. But, just as the German troops before them, the Russians re-occupied Budapest before dawn on a Sunday. And some 200,000 Hungarians undertook the long walk. In my case, it took two days and two nights of dodging checkpoints, military search lights, and potential minefields. At the end of it, in the dead of night, I met my first American. He jumped out from behind a haystack, brandishing a flashlight. He was one of countless American students who had formed a human chain to make sure that those who had made it across the zigzag frontier did not accidentally reenter Hungarian territory.

And so, eventually, I boarded the Pan Am DC-6 that brought me to these shores. Before, between the ages of eight and twenty, socialism's vocabulary (words, phrases, definitions) and socialism's repertory of tools (procedures, practices, mannerisms) had become etched on my brain. Party operatives spoke as if playing back a tape from a deck inside their skull, with the First Secretary changing the tape every time new directives came from Moscow. Every vile deed was done for the sake of "world peace." The source of all virtue was the Soviet Man; the source of all evil was the American Oppressor. Good people were *progressive*, bad people were *reactionary*—or was it the other way around: progressives were good people; reactionaries, bad? Those who misspoke had to engage in self-criticism and go into sensitivity training. If your father owned a small store, you could do no good. If your father worked in a factory, you could do no evil. To make certain your origins were not hidden, a large red letter identified your ancestry on every form attached to your record.

On April 20, 1964, the day I became American, I gave special thanks because all of that seemed forever behind me.

CHAPTER THREE

PATHWAY TO PANIC

THE YEARS OF unclouded joy were short.

During the late 1960s I watched in despair as my brilliantly gifted piano students suddenly began to speak as if someone had replaced *their* brains with prerecorded tapes. They spoke in phrases—repeated mechanically—which were neither the product of, nor accessible to, intelligent consideration. At first, these tapes seemed to contain only a few slogans about "love and peace." Fruitful conversation became impossible, but that was merely regrettable. The situation became alarming when the "tapes" began to include words and phrases that had become familiar to me in Hungary during the nazi and Soviet occupations, and which contributed to the reasons for my decision to escape. Worse yet, the words and phrases were soon followed by practices of similar pedigree.

"Reactionary," "exploitation," "oppressor and oppressed," and "redistribution" were some of the words taken straight from the Marxist repertoire. The term "politically correct" first came to my attention through the writings of Anton Semionovich Makarenko, Lenin's expert on education. Adolf Hitler preferred the version "socially correct." Then came the affirmative action forms which classified people by ancestry—first signed into law in Nazi Germany—and the preferential treatment of specific categories, introduced by the Stalinist government in 1950.

More than any single component, however, I was struck by the growing overall hostility toward long-standing American traditions and their English origins. Suggestions of reducing the central role of the English language soon followed. These developments brought to mind a strange similarity between certain actions of nazi and Soviet occupation forces. Both gave special significance to any contact with the English-speaking world, to the point where listening to an English-language broadcast was severely punished.

If nazis and communists—supposed opposites—agreed about their primary enemy, could there be further similarities? Thus began my search which, in time, led to the discovery of their common philosophical roots. Next, it became increasingly clear that most of the political positions people take derived from no more than two major sources of political thought with origins in only a few countries. Most importantly, persuasive evidence emerged about the sources of the doctrines that were replacing America's founding principles. Slowly, the chief protagonists and their long-standing conflict came into focus.

In the 1960s, for the first time, Americans became participants in that conflict, not on the field of battle—as in two world wars and the Cold War—but in their schoolrooms, boardrooms, and bedrooms. It added an entirely new and often confusing dimension to traditional disputes between Democrats and Republicans. The longer it went on, the more this age-old conflict between worldviews set the political agenda on both sides, to the point where party affiliation became secondary. Yet the real conflict was hidden behind an intricate web of "issues." The real conflict was well-nigh invisible. It remains invisible. And that is worrisome.

Brilliant and seasoned observers of the body politic have spoken of their respective concerns about judges who legislate, environmentalists who seem irrational, regulators who run amok, educators who deconstruct the reasons for education, new citizens who neither speak the language nor understand the basics of America, armed forces constantly under attack from within, quota systems that defy the Constitution, or the news and entertainment media's frequent contempt for America.

These pages will attempt to connect the many points of conflict that may appear separate, but are not. And what ultimately emerges as a single conflict is simply the continuation of a centuries-old one between two immensely powerful schools of thought.

This book, then, is about political ideas, their origins, and their consequences. The book is *not* about my personal like or dislike of countries or peoples. Given the frequent references to French and German political thought, it may be relevant to recall that, as a pianist, I have spent most of my waking hours in the company of Bach, Mozart, Beethoven, Schubert, Schumann, and Brahms. As for France, my wife and I visit there as often and for as long as possible. In other words, it is entirely feasible to admire everything but the political contributions of certain thinkers in a particular country; it is equally feasible to admire the political institutions in another country and not care much, say, about its food. Suggestions that everyone is equally wonderful in everything they do will not be found on these pages. Indiscriminate admiration is as meaningless as indiscriminate rejection.

Because the task of establishing the links and placing them in a broad context appeared more urgent than any other, I have not availed myself of too many detailed case histories which, though they would add further substance to the argument, have already appeared in newspapers, magazines, and books by distinguished authors. The chief purpose here is to present the "big picture," and my hope is that we may even dispense with the distinction between so-called culture wars and political ones, with the argument about values versus virtues, or the treatment of moral decline as a separate concern. Our woes, all of them, are inexorably connected.

THE PARTIES AND THE CONFLICT

Every day, serious persons tell us that "communism has lost," "socialism has collapsed," "conservatism is taking over America." Each of these is an inaccurate assumption, or the product of wishful thinking. For the past thirty years, all aspects of our lives—and all of our institutions—have been moving in one direction: away from America's founding principles. Like a compass, these principles—foremost among them the rule of law, individual rights, guaranteed property, and a common American identity—have provided our bearings for two centuries. And every time we move away from America's founding principles, we move in the direction of the sole realistic alternative.

That alternative is one we call by pseudonyms because we are reluctant to confront its proper label: communism—not in the sense of Stalin's gulag or Mao's Cultural Revolution, but as a logical end state where the objective of socialism, "social justice," has been achieved. As such, it continues to attract many.

We ought not to be afraid of the *word*. We ought properly to be terrified of the *world* it conjures up. At the same time, we ought to harbor great respect for "Communism: The Idea" which has survived cataclysmic "errors" and continues to enjoy the benefit and support of excellent minds. Just how much sympathy communism elicits today may be measured by the number of those—notably on America's college campuses and in the media—who categorically refuse to look upon communist societies and their victims the same way they look upon Nazi Germany and *its* victims. Additional confirmation may be found in the warmth and understanding with which America's own communists are portrayed.

The last three decades have produced a debate about the very nature—*the very existence*— of this nation. Unlike all previous political discourse, the question is a fundamental one: Is this country to remain the United States of America, pursuing the course of success as charted by America's Founders, or are the people ready to accept an entirely different type of society—based on alien ideas with a record of catastrophic failure?

Use of the word "alien" should not be construed as a protectionist posture. Rather, it points to the deeply held conviction—evolved over decades—that the traditional debate between Left and Right, Democrat and Republican, even liberal and conservative, circumvents the fundamental question, because the proposed alternative to "America-as-we-know-it" is of alien origin.

From the earliest beginnings, essential differences could be observed between English and French concepts of liberty, equality, and government. Those differences deepened as English thought became infused with, and enriched by, the Scottish Enlightenment, as well as by the contributions of the exceptionally inspired group of men we call the Founders of America. Simultaneously, French thought might have been consumed by the flames of the French Revolution of 1789 and its aftermath, had it not been taken up by a succession of the most ambitious thinkers in Germany.

And so, we speak of a "Franco-Germanic" side, and an "Anglo-American" side, risking accusations of ethnic stereotyping where none is intended. Why the insistence on designation? Because disregard of the true origin of political ideas and agendas will stand in the way of their proper evaluation. Because not knowing the origin of an idea, and the rationale behind it, allows advocates of that idea to hide its history, and to dress it in the attire of their choice. Honest discussions are hampered by the mistaken assumption that communism is Russian, or that communism and national socialism—nazism—are on opposite sides. Honest discussion is also hampered by camouflaging Franco-Germanic doctrine with traits that come naturally to Americans, such as caring and compassion.

At its simplest, the Franco-Germanic philosophical position may be characterized as attributing to human reason an unlimited capacity to comprehend, evaluate, and arrange the affairs of our world. Pursuant to this, the proper sequence in charting the future course for humanity calls for the theory to be developed first, and for people and events to conform to it. By contrast, the Anglo-American position regards human reason as bounded by limitations, and in need of moral guidance as it attempts to provide for the future. In this way of thinking, it is observation, experience, and lessons learned that form the basis of society's choice in organizing its institutions.

No area of human activity, no form of human interchange is unaffected by these fundamental differences. Since political thought functions as a foundation under, and as an umbrella over, all theaters of human activity, it reflects those same differences. To date, all applicable political thought has been the product of one or the other. A third possibility has yet to be articulated. Accordingly, on one side we find the perfect political theory and corresponding prescriptions which, it is claimed, will necessarily lead to the perfect society. In that perfect society, all will achieve perfect contentment. While no evidence as yet exists to prove the upside potential of this Franco-Germanic doctrine, the Soviet Union, Germany's Third Reich, and China's "Cultural Revolution" have demonstrated the downside. By contrast, Anglo-American thinkers have settled for limited, but attainable, goals. One of these was to extend the blessings of liberty to more people than was possible in other forms of society. Liberty, in turn, produced unprecedented accumulations of wealth, and increased access to it by a constantly growing number of people. We have seen the upside—it is called the United States of America.

Current political parlance refers to the two sides in a variety of ways. Of the first, "utopian," "statist," and "collectivist," are the tamer labels; "totalitarian" and "socialist" are the more aggressive. "Big government" is often used to skirt proper identification altogether. For the sake of clarity, I have settled on different designations. "Franco-Germanic" refers to the origins, "the search for social justice" to the method, and "communism" to the end state. Renewed confirmation of the end state comes from no less an authority than Jiang Zemin, president of the People's Republic of

China and head of China's—the world's largest—Communist Party. On September 12, 1997, using words identical to the ones I first encountered in 1949, he identified socialism as a transitory phase, and communism as the goal.

The other side is often called "capitalism" which, as we shall see, is a deliberate misnomer for free enterprise. This side is of Anglo-American origin, employs the rule of law as its method, and—although it acknowledges a number of aspirations and guiding principles—does not presume the existence of an end state.

If indeed only two major schools of political thought can be perceived, it stands to reason that they have taken consistently contrary positions. It is equally reasonable to assume that all major conflicts, though colored by additional participants and causes, have been clashes between the two schools. Both world wars, as well as the Cold War, fall in this category, as does the current debate about America's future.

Before the 1960s the United States was a participant only to the extent that it came to Britain's aid when necessary and, increasingly, assumed the position of chief defender of Anglo-American principles. As for the debate itself, America chose its path at the time of the Founding, rendering moot any further discussion of the fundamentals. There remained only questions of improved implementation, and that process provided political parties with plenty of ground on which to disagree. Franco-Germanic ideas have been propagated by progressives, New Dealers, and socialists, not to mention outright communists. Yes, the graduated income tax and social security put dents into traditional concepts of self-sufficiency. But until recently no assault had been waged on America as a nation, on America as a concept, on the fundamental tenets of Anglo-American political thought. The 1960s unleashed all three.

The 1960s unleashed all three, but carefully avoided identifying the chief protagonist. There was the yearning for "love and peace." There was the resistance to a "horrible and unfair" war in Vietnam.

There was an overdue civil rights movement, and there was an equally "overdue" sexual revolution. All these, the nation was led to believe, were consistent with traditional American aspirations. All these, the reasoning went, were consistent with the traditional debate about the implementation of American principles. The impatience of youth and the delay in the desegregation of black Americans may have produced an explosive mix, commentators mused, but different generations tend to be, well, different.

But if so, why the substitution of a "search for social justice" where once the law ruled? Why the proliferation of group privilege to the detriment of individual rights? Why the abolition of guaranteed property through regulation, redistribution, and entitlements? Why the daily assaults on our common American identity by hyphenation, bilingual ballots, multiculturalism, and phony history books?

Why? Because the overwhelming success of Anglo-American principles in society seemed to match the apparent Anglo-American invincibility on the field of battle. America was the "immovable object" standing in the way of the "irresistible force" socialist ideology must prove itself to be. Dislodging the immovable object necessitated that Americans participate in significant numbers. That, in turn, would be possible only if:

> (1) Americans were reminded frequently of their failures, and of various "wrongs" they and their country had inflicted on an ever-growing multitude
>
> (2) Americans were persuaded that all apparently new ideas were, in fact, old American ideas and that by acting in accordance with those, they would become "better Americans"
>
> (3) a constantly expanding range of people who had been "unfairly treated" and "deserving of special treatment" could be produced to keep the conscience of Americans troubled.

All three have come to pass. As a result, any suggestion that harm to America could be intended was made to sound preposterous. How can a "more perfect" implementation of "American ideals" possibly harm America?

The success of this campaign of deception is the compelling reason for hammering away at the *non-American* origin of the other side, and for placing the current debate about America's future in the context of centuries. Equally important is that we discover the connections that link hundreds or thousands of seemingly unconnected projects, campaigns, incidents, organizations, agendas, and publications that, together, constitute the all-out effort to transform America from top to bottom.

Still, there is good news as well, once we clarify the origin and nature of the protagonists. The good news is that choosing the American side has no bearing on a person's traditional political preferences. There has always been, there must always be, ample room for the resulting differences in the body politic. A healthy, dynamic society is hardly conceivable without them. And falling into the trap of Franco-Germanic ideas has not been an exclusive affliction of Democrats or liberals.

Better still, unlike other epidemics, this one may be arrested simply by a return to America's founding principles. Tens of millions still live by them, getting up every day to work, raise a family, and live the good life. They do their best to absorb the assault on their world, and they try to ignore the ominous signs that led to the conclusions on these pages.

These conclusions have not been prompted either by fantasies of "conspiracy," or by teenage "hang-ups." Nothing would please me more than to be proven wrong. A fruitful argument, however, is possible only between parties willing to face reality. Part of that reality is that we know of only one alternative to America's founding principles that has been worked out in any detail.

The alternative is the steady move toward communism, however

preposterous such a proposition may sound at a time when the Dow
Jones reaches new high after new high. While we toast the seemingly endless bull market, ominous changes are taking place in the
way we live. Before you dismiss the proposition out of hand, I ask for
some of your time so that, together, we may reconstruct the events
leading up to the scenario that is America today.

LAW

CHAPTER FOUR

ASPIRATIONS

MESSAGES FROM THE PAST

A remarkable similarity of motifs permeates the original epics—one might call them defining legends—handed down through the mists of time and recorded by early scribes. We encounter men who knew all and could do all, travels to distant places and magic deeds, women who had to be wooed, and riches beyond one's wildest dreams. Chivalry, rivalry, and the quest for power are recurring themes. The casual observer will point to the apparent sameness of humans, be they portrayed in the *Chanson de Roland* of the French, *Das Nibelungenlied* of the Germans, *Prince Igor* of the Russians, the *Kalevala* of the Finns, *The Epic of Gilgamesh* of the Sumerians, *Ramayana* of India, *Hiawatha* of the Onondaga, or the *Legend of the Magic Stag* that Hungarians learn in grade school.

These legends are repositories of a people's desires and aspirations. Through them, we learn about the possessions and attributes they value above all else. The more discerning reader will soon detect that some traveled solely to win wars, others also to gain knowledge. Some triumphed through personal valor, others preferred to employ magic. Women were prized for their beauty, or wealth, or both. One, Brünhilde of the Germans, was noted as well for her athletic prowess, which the suitor had to match.

England's legend of King Arthur contains many elements of the standard epic: war, and knights, and ladies, and Merlin the Enchanter. What is different, indeed unique, is that the participants sit at a *round* table—a table giving precedence to no one, not even the king. Whereas all other epics emphasize the greater ability and supreme accomplishment of the hero, thereby justifying the power and wealth possessed by him, some versions of the Arthurian legend speak of a round table that accommodates 1,600 people at a time. Whereas magic powers were attributed to many (Gilgamesh of the Sumarians, Väinämöinen of the Finns), only Merlin used his to build a one-of-a-kind gift for his king—the Round Table which embodies the most elusive aspiration of all: equality in the affairs of man.

While for the outside world the founding legend is representative of a people, it lives on to become a guiding influence in the life of a people—a constant source of names, events, allegories, and, again, desires and aspirations. The last two are quite different from one another. Desire seeks to be satisfied and fulfilled. Aspirations must be achieved. Desire tends to be basic and physical: a table of plenty laden with delicacies, the love of an attractive mate, an opulent home. Aspiration aims at the intangible, often at the spiritual. Fulfillment of a person's desire, in most instances, will affect the person only. Achievement of an aspiration is likely to affect others. To produce a superb meal is the achievement of aspiration. To eat it is the fulfillment of desire.

Yet this is not to suggest that aspirations are invariably noble manifestations of the human spirit when compared to desires. As opposed to the writing of *Hamlet* or the Ninth Symphony, aspiration for power may—and usually does—have disastrous consequences for others. But there is a significant distinction, because desire is by nature passive, while aspiration is active.

The initial activity takes the form of *thinking*. And here, again, is an important distinction: desires surface through the senses, and provoke feelings of various sorts. The thought process that gives birth to aspirations develops independently of sensory needs. Aspirations reflect the thought processes of countless generations and are deeply embedded in the consciousness of a people. As the origins go back a long way, so the achievement requires vast expanses of time.

In short, before the deed, there must be thought. Before the achievement, there must be aspiration. The symbolism of the round table reflects a deep yearning for equality. The realization of equality depends upon a rule of law which grants precedence to no one, and which all must obey.

THE BIRTH OF LIBERTY

The legend of King Arthur has Welsh origins, and owes much in its final form to medieval French contributions. Yet its most unusual component, the Round Table, found its permanent home in the souls of Englishmen. A century-and-a-half after the Norman invaders joined forces with the Anglo-Saxons to establish a nation, Arthur's Round Table bore eternal fruit. In the year 1215, during the month of June, a meeting took place at Runnymede to hammer out the covenants that would be forced down the throat of weak King John. Merlin had used magic and given Arthur the Round Table as a present. The barons and churchmen of England used their superior power and created a system of laws which became a model for mankind. Their aspiration—to secure advantages for people other than themselves—elevates the authors of the Magna Carta, the great charter of English liberties, to true nobility.

A few clauses of Section III of the Magna Carta are of particular interest. Clause 39 asserts that "no freeman shall be taken or imprisoned, or disseised, or outlawed, or exiled, or in any way destroyed, nor will we go upon him, nor will we send upon him, except by the lawful judgment of his peers, or by the law of the land." Clause 40: "To no one will we sell, deny or delay right or justice." Clause 42 declares all persons are to be free to come and go, and stay in the land in time of peace except outlaws, prisoners, and enemy aliens. Section V, Clause 38, adds: "No bailiff in his own bare word without credible witness is to send a man to the ordeal." Other clauses deal with the measure of fines which must fit, and not exceed, the crime and which must not deprive anyone of his livelihood.

Again, the year was 1215, or 1223 if we look to the version whose wording exercised the greatest influence on eighteenth-century America. Genghis Khan had invaded China, his successors were rolling over Russia and preparing to invade Europe. The Germans of the Holy Roman Empire were doing constant battle against the papacy and the Church, while France attempted to steer a middle course. While the Golden Horde of the Mongols plotted the conquest of the known world, Europeans were organizing one crusade after another to liberate the Holy Land. Islam under Saladin began its thrust both North and West, slowly preparing for its own most forceful attempt to subjugate Europe. The scene was made yet more colorful by an infinite number of local skirmishes among feudal lords of higher or lower standing. Kings, princes, and barons aspired to gain territory, to secure income, to organize the administration of their lands, to consolidate their rule.

Some aspired to build great cathedrals and castles and palaces, to develop great centers of learning, to establish legal processes through which disputes could be resolved at regular intervals. The centers of learning usually explored questions of theology, or the relationship between theology and secular thought. The delivery of justice was subject to the will of local rulers or, occasionally, to certain remnants of Roman law. A fully developed, Roman-based legal system was centuries away on the Continent of Europe and, even then, frequent changes in the law made a mockery of the very concept. For centuries to come, many places did not even pretend to have a system of laws.

Placed thus in the proper historic context, the significance of the Magna Carta emerges in its full glory. It is a gigantic step toward achieving the unique aspiration expressed in the symbolism of the Round Table. While all rulers—great and small, urban and rural, sophisticated and nomadic—looked to secure power *over* everyone in sight, the authors of the great charter *subordinated* the king, their posterity, and, most important of all, themselves to its provisions. Were they that much better, wiser, nobler than anyone else? No, they had merely arrived at a simple truth: *A person's rights are best secured by conceding the very same rights to every other person under the same jurisdiction.*

The great charter of 1215, and its subsequent versions, meant neither the achievement of a state of instant perfection nor the end of the debate. Centuries of internal strife, bloodshed, and trial and error were to follow. But, in England, yardsticks had been laid down and aspirations clearly articulated many centuries before people in other countries would even begin to think about the fundamental matters that the charter set forth once and for all. Other great cultures in which the arts and sciences flourished—where aspirations of the human spirit brought forth buildings, books, paintings, and music of immense beauty, where knowledge of the world grew at an ever-increasing pace—have failed to discover the simple concept of *reciprocal* rights. Legal scholars of distinction produced writings to fill several libraries, yet this seemingly obvious prescription for domestic tranquility escaped their attention. The object of their aspiration was order—not fairness to all.

Fairness is an English word. It was, it *is*, an English concept.

CROSSING THE ATLANTIC

The most precious cargo brought ashore by the people who arrived on North America's eastern coast took up no space on those tiny ships. It consisted of memories of the Round Table and the promises of the great charter. Both now formed but a part of a whole new set of aspirations.

No doubt England was fortunate in being spared foreign invasions and in developing a national character that was joined at the hip to the concept of liberty. And the world was fortunate that thirteen English colonies made up the core of what was to become the United States of America. The ways of these English colonists, soon to be called "Americans," was so attractive that it drew Scottish, Irish, German, and Dutch settlers, all of whom blended in with ease. Most arrivals were people who wanted to achieve, and who were willing to pay the price of achieving. In consequence, compared with other societies, the colonists made up the greatest conceivable density of highly motivated individuals. They were, in short, "people with aspirations."

At the same time, many were transported to America unwillingly, with no wish to be pioneers in a strange new land. As we shall see, that—more than skin color or the long years of slavery—produced the divisions that were to haunt this nation.

But during the seventeenth and eighteenth centuries, an increasingly stable, healthy, and prosperous society, whose achievements were to impress the world, took root. The new "Americans" lived by respect for the law—God's law, which they habitually read in the Bible, and the man-made laws which, they knew, were the guarantors of their liberty. And when the "present English King"—as the Declaration of Independence refers to George III—broke the law, they marshaled the strength to take stock, clean house, and articulate their own set of aspirations. They created a model that would inspire and guide the world. And an American, Thomas Jefferson, crafted the phrase that would express the greatest aspiration of which human beings are capable. He held this truth to be self-evident, "that all men are created equal."

CHAPTER FIVE

ON THE EQUALITY OF HUMANS

FACT OR GOAL?

The reverberations of Jefferson's defining phrase have reached the far corners of the earth, but interpretations tend to obfuscate its extraordinary assumption. Some look upon it as a statement of fact, others as a magic wand that instantly creates the condition it described. All these have been disappointed, but the fault lies not with Jefferson's phrase.

Profound, inspiring, and glorious as the phrase is, it would be nothing more than a phrase, had not a growing number of people come to agree with its premise, and had not conditions been established to fulfill its promise.

The phrase can express but a belief, a yearning, a purpose and, yes, an aspiration. One would have had to be unrealistic not to notice that, in 1776, only a small minority of humans would have agreed. One would have had to be arrogant to presume that, among all inhabitants of this planet, the signatories of the Declaration of Independence alone were privy to divine insight. No, the Founding Fathers were both realists and humble. They identified a goal. Pointing a path is the *first step toward*, not the arrival at, that goal.

Many believe that the phrase encompasses a great deal more than it actually says about equality, for even a cursory glance reveals among people a bewildering range of physical characteristics, of muscular ability and intellectual capacity, of accomplishment, of means at their disposal. The incontrovertible fact is that people appear to be unequal in all those aspects that affect our senses, in all those that we can measure. Did Jefferson fool himself, or did he set out to fool others?

Certainly not, if we are willing to meet his reasoning with our own. He wrote: "We hold these truths to be self-evident...." In this usage, *Webster's Dictionary* tells us, "hold" means "to abide by a promise," "to keep inviolate as a faith." Jefferson knew that those truths were far from self-evident in most quarters, or there would have been no need to place them at the head of the Declaration. If we see the phrase as an expression of faith, as an aspiration, as a promise, we will not waste our time on divisive polemics. And if we cease to read the word "equal" as if it meant "the same," we will have removed a main impediment to successful realization. "Equal" refers to *standing*; "same" would imply that we were all clones.

As the new millennium approaches, confusion seems to be growing. The most vocal advocates of "celebrating our diversity" insist simultaneously that people are the same everywhere. Activists who extol the "individual genius" of every human being insist that there is no difference between two individuals, between two cultures, between two civilizations. That is not what Thomas Jefferson had in mind. He was no fool. "May [the choice we made] be the signal of arousing men to burst the chains under which monkish ignorance and superstition had persuaded them to bind themselves," he wrote in his last extant letter.

In appearance, people can be tall or short, thin or fat, blond or brown, handsome or plain. Some can swim fast, others can jump high; some can assemble a model airplane, others cannot change a light bulb; some can hear a train in the distance, others can't tell if the phone rings in the next room. Is it reasonable to assume that—although different in every other aspect—we have the same mental, intellectual abilities? To a building contractor who needs a plumber, a concert pianist will not be of equal value. To an orchestra looking for a soloist, a plumber will be of no value at all. Mundane examples? It is precisely because people's appearances, abilities, and station in life are so different that the aspiration for equality welled up in those souls of old. It is precisely because people's appearances, abilities, and station in life are so different that, of all aspirations, this is the most elusive—and the most exalted.

Among the attributes which render one person different from another, aspiration is decisive. One who is possessed by it will act differently from the one who is not. A group, a society, a nation in which a critical mass of its members is possessed by it will act differently from those that are not. Not necessarily better, but differently. For one thing, whatever the balance sheet of a person or a nation, there are likely to be more entries on it.

BALANCE SHEETS OF HISTORY

Balance sheets, for the present purpose, refer to that compendium of personal or collective characteristics, accomplishments, failures, and a miscellany of other "credits" and "debits" which individuals and identifiable groups of individuals build up over time, and which accompany us, like it or not. The faster the pace of our lives, the more we depend on that balance sheet for quick decisions. Weighing decisions about marriage or employment represent extreme cases. But we consider balance sheets every time we invite a person to our home, choose a place of vacation, or purchase a pizza. And how else would we make our decisions at the ballot box?

Balance sheets may be personal or historical. Historical balance sheets—if they are known, and they come into play only if they are known—are made up mostly of contributions to humanity on the

positive side, and of suffering inflicted upon humanity on the negative side of the ledger. For example, over the centuries England has
inflicted much suffering upon, and taken liberally from, the peoples
who happened to be under its physical control. So, too, has Spain.
But England has contributed so much to humanity in general, and
to the peoples under its control in particular, that its balance sheet is
overwhelmingly positive. The same cannot be said of Spain—which
explains much about the divergent courses and fortunes of North
and South America.

A more recent example is Serbia. Along with their widely
reported atrocities, the balance sheet of Serbians includes the entry
that, in their region, they alone stood up to both Hitler and Stalin.
Europe's reluctance to punish the atrocities may reflect memories of
Serbian grit when it counted. The fact is, because generalizations
have been used as the pretext for classifying and subsequently killing
millions, we now pretend balance sheets do not exist. In reality, once
they penetrate our consciousness, they are there to stay. And, while
completely one-sided "accounts" are rare, there is a bottom line
which we see as positive or negative.

On an individual level, every person who is looking for employment or quality housing has to submit a resume (or application) and
references. Because resumes are heavily weighted to present the
"credit" side, employers hope that the references will at least hint at
any serious entries on the "debit" side. On a national level, we might
look to consumer products. Given the choice between Albanian and
Swiss chocolate, we find that the Swiss balance sheet on chocolate is
overwhelmingly positive, the Albanian is blank. Given the choice
between an American and a Russian airplane, we will choose the
American. In this we are not swayed by patriotism or industrial standards alone. The knowledge that human life is held more sacred in
America than in Russia forms a vital part of the balance sheet.

Proof of the importance of balance sheets may be found in the
attention paid to them by political activists. Historians, for example,

have taken aim at America's balance sheet. Publications deceptively labeled *National Standards for United States History*, and *National Standards for World History* represent an all-out effort to demean, diminish, or denigrate as many entries on the "credit" ledger of the United States and of western civilization as possible. This is supplemented by inventing credit entries on the balance sheets of others, and by constructing new, fictitious balance sheets where none existed.

I first encountered the practice of fictitious balance sheet entries while growing up in Hungary under the Stalinist regime. Having been taught before the Soviet occupation that the steam engine had been invented by James Watt, we students thought we could answer the question when posed by our new science teacher. Before he finished the question we shouted, "James Watt!" The poor man turned every color of the rainbow before clearing his throat and saying, "No—it was Polzunov." Later, we found out that all teachers had to undergo instant reeducation through which they were informed that everything had been invented, discovered, and devised by a Russian.

Tampering with the balance sheets was also evident during the recent commemorations by American television networks of Victory-in-Europe (VE) Day. Many of the programs focused on the efforts of the Red Army without so much as a mention of the American and British servicemen whose graveyards cover the coasts of Belgium and France as far as the eye can see. And, of course, affirmative action is the crudest application of collective balance sheets—real and artificial. Imagine a case in which the white son of Eastern-European immigrants, who barely survived the nazi concentration camps or the gulag, competes for admission or employment with the daughter of, say, a successful black businessman. Because some whites used to keep slaves six generations ago, and because many blacks were slaves six generations ago, the choice is made in favor of the latter, regardless of merit.

Such improper applications, indeed abuses, of balance sheets should not, however, diminish their validity. They are indispensable both in personal and in professional interaction. If every decision we make had to be based on a fresh evaluation of the pros and cons, we could not manage our affairs at all. That is, our dependence on balance sheets is entirely appropriate. What our conscience should not tolerate is the detrimental, exclusionary impact of collective balance sheets—real or imaginary—upon individuals. Such acts are rightly labeled as prejudicial. And prejudice is prejudice, whether applied to black or white, man or woman. Prejudice is abhorrent. But, in our effort to eradicate its negative effect on fellow humans, we have come to distort reality in our usage of the word. Increasingly, we cry "prejudice!" in situations where the operative component is *post*-judice—judgment *after* the fact, not before.

POST-JUDICE

Our preference for Swiss chocolate, American airplanes, French wines, or English common law is a matter of post-judice. Post-judice is empirical evidence acquired for oneself, and through others whose judgment we have found trustworthy. If a country has been known to produce quality merchandise, the label "made in..." will sell the new products of that country as well.

Post-judice alone permits prudent use of limited resources. How else would we know what "the best value for the money" happens to be? How else would we know not to buy a vacuum cleaner with a history of frequent breakdowns? And, if post-judice is legitimate in terms of *things*, why not in terms of *people*? Surely, people build a record of competence, dependability, eagerness—or the contrary.

Intelligent realignment of these concepts is important because of the incessant attempts to legislate what is essentially a human process. By labeling many legitimate cases of post-judice "discrimination," sinister motives are inferred and punitive consequences prescribed. Would we hire piano movers who can barely lift empty boxes? Should we pay for someone with poor coordination to be trained for the U.S. Open tennis championships? And, if physical characteristics are so different, how about intellectual ones? Must we *see* differences before we believe they exist?

One person's mental or intellectual ability can be vastly different from another's. Those who deny this are inflicting irreversible damage upon the dynamic properties of a healthy society. What special brand of arrogance leads someone to declare that, while people may be tall or short, strong or weak, intellectually all have the identical potential? The idea had to be planted in people's consciousness. It certainly did not get there as the result of observation.

EGALITY VS. EQUALITY

"Égalité, Fraternité, Liberté" or "Egality, Fraternity, Liberty"—these were the slogans the French Revolution of 1789 emblazoned on its banner. Much of Europe was intoxicated by the event, and to this day, in many a land, schoolchildren are told to look upon it as the great wave of liberation that swept across the European continent. Because the French gave us the Statue of Liberty, many Americans, too, make the mistaken assumption that liberty has French origins.

Note that I translate the French slogan "Égalité" as "Egality," and not as "Equality." *Webster's Dictionary* tells us that egality is "an extreme social and political leveling." Our word "egalitarian" confirms that definition. The process of leveling is worlds apart from equality in the affairs of man, which was the aspiration of the Round Table. Nothing illustrates the point more graphically than the instrument, used indiscriminately by the French, to accomplish this leveling. If someone's head appeared to stand out, it was simply chopped off by the guillotine. Enforced egality became the primary tool applied to the living by those who made themselves masters of life and death. In the twentieth century, would-be dictators attended what might facetiously be called the "Vladimir Ilyich Lenin School of Population and Behavior Control," but Lenin himself learned from the French Revolution how to force everyone to be the same.

Customarily, revolutions conjure up images of destruction, bloodshed, turmoil, mass hysteria, the complete breakdown of civil order, and the rise of the roughest and loudest to the highest positions. This would accurately describe the events of the French Revolution. More importantly: *de*struction was not followed by *con*struction. A pattern was established, and it led in a straight line from Paris, 1789, to the staple phrase of liberalism in present-day America: we must *eliminate*.... Then, it was "the privilege of the aristocracy and the clergy." Now, it is "racism," "hunger," "hate," or "the glass ceiling." The American Revolution was an entirely different type of event; it is more accurately called the War of Independence. Yes, blood was shed, and a break with the existing ruler was made. But the bloodshed was confined to combatants, and far more important was the ensuing construction—the *creation* of lasting institutions, which never came to pass in France. The designation of France today is "Fifth Republic," with as many and more attempts at a constitution.

Egality is the elimination of differences. Since people *are* different, only force can cover up the differences, and then only temporarily. Once force is no longer applied, the differences reappear. This is the result of different attributes, different aspirations, and the resulting different balance sheets. Nations, too, can be forced to exist on a level they had long surpassed. That was Russia's crime when it forced its considerably lower state of civilization upon its Western neighbors. But as soon as the Red Army departed, the historic qualities of Prague and Budapest reemerged. Their long-standing balance sheets came into play almost instantaneously.

America's balance sheet is exceptionally rich and positive, partly as a result of its demographic composition. Different countries harbor variable proportions of people with aspirations—from near-zero to very high. But all who undertook the journey to America from the four corners of the world had aspirations of some kind, making America's "aspiration density" the highest in the world. It would be higher still, had all newcomers undertaken the journey of their own free will. But that was not the case. And that, more than any other single factor, caused a rift that time alone will heal.

Thomas Jefferson could not have failed to note the differences that render people unequal. And because he observed that political institutions elsewhere made people *permanently* unequal, he placed his faith in a political creation. He hoped to set this nation—and through it, the world—on a path that could free everyone of the impediments of inequality. He, and others of his persuasion, believed that we are equal in the eyes of God. But precisely because we appear unequal in every other respect, it is only in the eyes of the law that we may become equal on earth. He, and others of his persuasion, realized that if a permanent framework of fundamental law were to be applied equally, living within such a framework would unlock individual potential to the fullest. *Equality would be achieved in the sense that every person could rise to the highest level which that person's talent, industry, and aspiration allowed.*

Nothing needed to be eliminated but the obstacles in the way of the individual.

Institutions and guarantees needed to be *established* so that citizens could not be denied the opportunity to achieve their highest possible status in society and, once achieved, it could not be taken away. That is equality in the practical sense.

In order to secure such conditions, the legal framework had to be fair. The legal framework had to be constant. The legal framework had to permit no exceptions.

This we call the Rule of Law.

CHAPTER SIX

WHOSE LAW?

LIVING WITHOUT LAW

In the 1970s, a true story made the rounds in Soviet-occupied Budapest. The subject of the story was a celebrated star of the Hungarian State Opera who had a chronically ill, bed-ridden brother. Every Friday afternoon from two to six, the singer sat at his brother's bedside. Every Friday afternoon, year in, year out, he parked his car in the same spot.

On the Friday in question, he came back to his car at six o'clock and found the huge notice of a fine glued (literally) to his windshield. The singer was baffled. He looked around for a policeman. One happened to be nearby. He walked over to the officer. "I'm glad to see you!" the singer exclaimed. "This is a mistake." "No mistake," said the patrolman. "You were parked in a no-parking zone." "But I have been parking here for years," protested the star. "Do you see this sign?" asked the keeper of the law. "It clearly says: parking not permitted."

The singer looked. The sign was unmistakable. "Officer," said our hero, "I swear by everything sacred, that sign was not here at two o'clock when I arrived." "Right you are," said the voice of authority.

41

"It was placed here at 4 PM—I held it myself while they poured the concrete around it. That will be 600 florins."

As in Italy, opera stars enjoy special status in Budapest. Our singer decided to refuse the fine, and got on the phone to see who among his friends would know a police officer of higher rank and of proven operatic taste. A colonel was identified, and the appointment made. True to expectations, the colonel could not stop talking about all the wonderful performances for which he felt indebted to our singer. He then listened to the story and shook his head in disbelief. "Let me check it out," the colonel offered, "and come back to see me next week."

The following week, the star showed up at the colonel's office with a confident grin. The colonel, too, was grinning. "I looked into it," he said, still shaking his head, "and it happened exactly as you said. They put up the sign while you were sitting at the bedside of your sick brother." He got up and stretched out a hand. "You are 100 percent right. Pay only 300 florins!"

This lighthearted story introduces a topic of exceptional gravity. Because people in the United States have never had to endure the absence of law, they have little perception about what people elsewhere have to contend with every day. In the vast majority of places the concept of a written, systematic law has never been known, or only recently has been introduced. Communities or societies in which the chief or the elders sit down to pass judgment offer no basis for comparison. Neither custom, nor the power of the leader, nor even the wisdom of the most mature members has anything to do with law as we understand it. In order to appreciate fully what the American system of laws offers we have to look to advanced societies whose sophistication is comparable to ours in most other aspects of life.

This, by necessity, takes us to Europe. And, before proceeding further, we might as well deal with the contemporary obsession to persecute what certain people label as "Eurocentrism." (It is a detour, but a necessary detour.) Since the 1960s, a significant number of Europeans, and Americans of European origin, have engaged in what must be an historic first: declaring their own western civilization irrelevant. They wish to discontinue it. Paradoxically, participants in broad-based education who come from Asia, Africa, South America, or Oceania, have to attend the great schools of western civilization to learn about themselves—let alone about others. Has contemporary academia asked itself where they will go? Where will anybody go?

It is fascinating to watch the quarrel "anti-Eurocentrics" have with God, Nature, or whomever they credit with the creation of man. Whose "fault" is it that some people, and the communities they formed, turned out to be more inquisitive than others? To have aspirations others did not have? And would the anti-Eurocentrics be prepared to live anywhere *outside* western civilization? Would they be willing to forego that which they condemn? Would Vice President Al Gore of the United States, who believes the automobile is evil, ride a horse to the Old Executive Office Building?

A REVIEW OF BASICS

To resume our discussion of law: there are three great divisions. The primary division is between societies that have no established legal structure and those that have. A second division is between the legal systems of western civilization—wherever adopted—and all others. And last, within the western models, we distinguish between systems based on Roman law, and systems based on English or common law. In this respect, the dividing line has been the English Channel—that "moat defensive to a house, Against the envy of less happier lands," as Shakespeare refers to it in *Richard II*.

Legal attitudes and traditions outside Western Civilization, where fundamentally different views of human conduct and interaction prevail, are beyond the scope of the present inquiry. The legends in Arabic, Persian, Chinese, and other Asiatic traditions of great and wise men, whose judgments became celebrated tales, tell of the dependence for justice on an exceptional individual. That is the antithesis to our concept of law which is held to preexist—and to provide guidance for—any judge. Our system thus liberates the matter at issue from the whim and disposition of the person sitting on the bench.

Western legal concepts continue in many parts to be viewed as "strange," as much in Saudi Arabia as in the People's Republic of China or Zaire. Keep this in mind when representatives from these and other lands stand before American news cameras and parrot phrases—"human rights," "free markets," "threats to the environment"—that they know will impress American viewers.

Our inquiry, then, is confined to the continent of Europe, and only to certain parts of it, for even in Europe several countries are latecomers to the very concept of law. The comparisons serve to illuminate relevant points and will also emphasize the rare and immense gift America's founders bequeathed to the nation.

In broad terms, Roman law refers to the concepts and institutions developed in and for the city, republic, or empire of ancient Rome. These concepts and institutions continued to determine legal proceedings after the fall of the Western Empire in the fifth century, and after the fall of the Eastern Empire in the fifteenth century AD. Roman law became the foundation and determining influence in some places which had never been part of the Roman Empire, Germany being a prime example. Indeed, legal categories and concepts present an excellent illustration of the difference between *power* and *influence*, which are frequently confused. The power of Rome disappeared a long long time ago. Rome's influence will be with us as long as there remains an "us."

Roman law went through many transmutations. The most lasting version bore the designation *Corpus Juris* (the "Body of the Law") which, by the eighteenth century, formed the basis of legal proceedings in much of Continental Europe. During the years following the revolution of 1789, the last monumental "renaissance" of Roman law occurred in France—the "Code Napoléon." In its fundamentals, and in the arrangement of its provisions, it owes a great deal to Roman law. The original Roman entity, the German adaptation of the *Corpus Juris*, and the Napoleonic Code are all supreme examples of the human intellect at its most brilliant. They, and their many derivatives, represent the aspirations of their authors to constrain the role of brute force and caprice in the affairs of man, and to create a framework for dependable guidance in the settlement of disputes.

These systems of law address a vast array of conditions, dealing with persons, property, and contract. With regard to persons, they tend to prescribe in some detail how individuals and families are expected to live and interact. The provisions reflect the application of learned thought, and the intent to give posterity the benefit of the best minds in guiding both jurists and other members of society through the trials and tribulations of disagreement. The provisions are "before the event," in other words independent of any actual occurrence, and are intended to govern all subsequent events. They depend for their administration on learned, professional jurists. To conjure up a ridiculously simplified image: in a dispute, turn to the appropriate paragraph of the law codes and find instructions for its proper resolution.

A system of laws is a prerequisite of civilized existence. Roman law was successful in protecting persons and property during times of peace, under stable conditions. Compared with the misery of most people living under most other systems, or no system at all, Roman law allowed periods of prosperity and periods of increased freedom.

Where Roman law broke down consistently on the European Continent was in the transition of power. And what it never quite delivered was the freedom of movement.

During the centuries of feudalism, the transfer of power depended on royal dynasties, princes, and warring nobility. Thus, the Napoleonic Code was intended to incorporate all the achievements of the French Revolution of 1789 and erase the legal vestiges—and with it, supposedly, all past ills—of feudalism. France has nonetheless gone through a number of subsequent revolutions and, to date, no fewer than five incarnations of the Republic. Most others have fared worse still. With regard to freedom of movement, it may be argued that as long as a person's address has to be registered with the police, it is restricted. There are degrees, of course. In Russia, as recently as 1991, freedom of movement did not exist.

On the other hand, the Magna Carta established freedom of movement in the English-speaking world as far back as 1215. The peaceful transition of power took a few additional centuries, but it, too, came to be. And the systems of laws west of the English Channel that sprang from those awesome beginnings were quite different from the Roman traditions of the continent. In England, it came to be known as the common law and, instead of expecting events to conform to precepts, it looked to actual precedents as it built a body of judicial opinions, case upon case. Simply stated, it relied on experience and common sense, as opposed to theory. Rather than restricting the practice of law to the closed ranks of professional jurists, common law invited every member in a given society to participate through the jury system.

AMERICA'S PRIMARY SOURCES

The founders of this nation had a vast panorama of intellectual riches before them. From antiquity came Greek philosophy, Roman law, and the Old and New Testaments of the Bible. From Europe came the great reformers of the Church: Luther, Calvin, and Zwingli; the writings of the French Enlightenment: Diderot, Montesquieu, Voltaire, and Rousseau; some great minds of old from Italy and the Netherlands—Aquinas, Erasmus—and, increasingly, from Germany. All were noted, all played a part, all entered the thought processes of America's founders. But the sole book that originated beyond the English Channel, and which they retained in its entirety, was the Bible. The significance of that is often lost in the turbulent discussions about the "separation of church and state."

For secular law, political philosophy, and the attributes of government, the founders looked to Britain. To some extent, this was a natural consequence of the language they spoke, the language that transmitted to them the stories, lessons, and parables of the Bible— the language of their education and orientation, which was, of course, English. Yet it would be unwise to underrate their conscious choice of those English institutions which, for a long time, had increasingly contained central power in favor of individual rights. America's founders recognized that these, rather than slogans, were the real ingredients of freedom. They read John Locke, whose *Essay concerning Human Understanding* and whose writings on natural law, political philosophy, toleration, and on the functions of government, determined the outlook of countless generations. During the years immediately preceding the founding, an embarrassment of intellectual riches became available in the histories of David Hume and Edward Gibbon; the legal *Commentaries* of William Blackstone; and the defining economic insights of Adam Smith, whose *Wealth of Nations* was published just months before the Declaration of Independence.

The Declaration, that most remarkable of documents, lists complaints against "the present King of Great Britain." Yet it leaves no doubt about the author's continuing admiration for "the free System of English Laws," and, in fact, uses it as a reason for the break with the mother country. The point is worth considering because of the ongoing debate about the nature of 1776. Some see it as a war of independence that did not affect the continuity of fundamental principles. Others insist on its revolutionary nature, stressing that the choice of a republican form of government, as well as the decision against any form of state religion, outweigh the traditions inherited from England.

WAS THERE AN AMERICAN REVOLUTION?

No doubt, these were choices of great consequence. Yet, when we say "revolution," we think of a "sudden, radical, complete change," not just according to *Webster's Dictionary*, but according to established usage of the word. In retrospect, none of the three words withstands scrutiny when applied to the founders. Theirs was an act of the most thoughtful consideration and deliberation of the human condition as far back as the eye could see. Their decisions were not born in the frenzy of the barricades, but in the minds of learned and civilized men. The principles they examined, amended, and affirmed reflected the thoughts and experiences that had stood the test of countless centuries.

Is that the stuff of which "radical and complete change" is made? Surely not. Our vision has been clouded by the proximity in time of the French Revolution, the tendency of certain historians to connect the two, and the undeniable influence that some aspects of French ideas and French events exerted upon the thinking of Jefferson and others.

Yet the differences appear to be far more decisive than the similarities. The French were literally destroying their existing internal order; Americans, while shaking off the rule of a monarch who had become "foreign," merely formalized a way of life much of which had already been established de facto. The French continued to lunge from crisis to crisis because they did not create lasting political institutions; Americans created institutions which were to withstand all manner of assaults from without and from within. The French were eager to export their revolution; Americans focused their attention on importing the best tools with which to create stability.

Most importantly, the founders did not consider their work finished with the Declaration of Independence. It was but a first step.

DRAWING THE AMERICAN MAP

Pronouncements about "unalienable Rights," government by the "consent of the governed," affirmation of "the Laws of Nature" and of "Nature's God," were indispensable ingredients of the future nation. They, as indeed all aspects of the document, pointed the path along which the new nation was to proceed. But beyond the political break with Great Britain, the founders' eyes were fixed on a future that, in retrospect, would have to justify that break. The history of those who embark on new paths without an adequate road map is a history of disastrous consequences.

By late 1786 George Washington joined the growing ranks of those who held that pointing the path would not, by itself, provide the foundations upon which to build a secure future for the nation. "What security has a man of Life, Liberty or Prosperity?" Washington asked. "Let us look to our National character, and to things beyond the present period." Indeed, the proclamation of unalienable rights to life, liberty, and the pursuit of happiness in and of itself does not—cannot—guarantee those blessings. Moreover, at that time, those rights were self-evident to few. Only a system of laws could secure them for all. And that system needed to be anchored in a document of uncommon durability. That document would be the road map with which to follow the path.

That document is known as the Constitution of the United States. Nothing like it had ever existed. It was unique in the public deliberation that led to its adoption; unique in the brevity and simplicity for a document of such immeasurable significance; unique in the influence it acquired and has held in the hearts and minds of freedom-loving people around the world.

The framers of the Constitution understood the wisdom of making few laws. The fewer the laws, the broader the agreement. The broader the agreement, the less need for enforcement. The less enforcement, the less friction between government and the governed. And the less friction, the less waste of time and energy. The time and energy thus freed vastly increases people's creative capacity.

That, in a nutshell, is the success story of the United States of America.

The brevity of the Constitution may have an additional explanation. As noted, the Bible was the common denominator among all those who came together to frame the supreme *secular* law of the land. The founders understood that the faith, morality, and ethics embodied in God's law should form the basis of all man-made laws. And Americans everywhere understood that the Rule of Law should form the basis of the new nation. Whereas in Europe the church steeple had long been the focal point of towns and villages, in the communities of America the courthouse became the town center.

DECLARATION VS. CONSTITUTION

Along with the debate about the nature of 1776—a war of independence or outright revolution?—is another debate that pits the Declaration of Independence against the Constitution as the defining document. Here the metaphor of the path and the road map will be helpful. And the Federalist Papers can be described as a glossary to the road map. Not least because of the orderly manner in which the Constitution may be amended, the three together have withstood every manner of upheaval from both within and without.

Europe, by contrast, continued to be the hothouse of ideas, in continuous state of fermentation. The French went from one revolution to another—1789, 1830, and 1848—the latter engulfing much of Europe. The Germans and Italians battled to establish national unity, and in 1871 became "Germany" and "Italy" at last, but not before another bloody round between the French and the Prussians. Next came the first world war, and the Bolshevik revolution of 1917 for which the seeds had been germinating since 1848. But the upheavals came and went. Neither bolshevism in Russia, nor fascism in Italy, nor national socialism in Germany seriously affected the United States because the Rule of Law stood guard, causing the giant waves of insanity to break on America's eastern seashore.

Domestic earthquakes were absorbed with equal success. What other legal-political structure could withstand a civil war, the assassinations of leaders at critical moments, and a crippling depression? Yet all turmoil, foreign and domestic, passed without affecting the path, the course upon which the United States had embarked, Americans protected their Constitution, and the Constitution protected America.

Then, sometime in the 1960s, a serious challenge was issued to the Rule of Law. The concept behind the challenge had been around for a long time. Antecedents of it can be found as far back as the Bible. But in the United States of America it never presumed to replace the supreme law of the land. In the United States of America, it never attempted to alter a way of thinking that had proved impervious to assaults and threats of all kind.

The challenger called itself "social justice."

CHAPTER SEVEN

"SOCIAL JUSTICE"

A MONUMENTAL DECEPTION

The quotation marks in the title are used advisedly. The words themselves are among the most successful deceptions ever conceived. Ask a variety of people to define what "social justice" means, specifically, and you will get as many answers as people queried. Ask the same person at different times and you will get different responses. All "definitions" of social justice boil down to any of the following:

> (1) somebody should have the power to determine what you can have, or
> (2) somebody should have the power to determine what you can*not* have, or
> (3) somebody should have the power to determine what to take away from you in order to give it to others who receive it without any obligation to earn it.

If millions upon millions have been deluded into searching for "social justice," it is because "social justice" displays the irresistible charm of the temptress and the armament of the enraged avenger;

because it adorns itself in intoxicating clichés and wears the insignia of the highest institutions of learning. Like a poisonous snake, it radiates brilliant colors. Like the poppies in *The Wizard of Oz*, it lulls the mind to sleep.

The easiest targets happen to be civilized people, who care about the fate of others. Americans, especially, are famous for their concern for fellow humans and support of worthy causes. They have fought two world wars to rescue western civilization, without any thought to material gain. Americans may be said to possess an uncommonly active "social" conscience. Actually, the word "conscience" does well enough alone. Why do we attach the word "social?"

Because, more than a century ago, advocates of socialism embarked on a campaign to inject the word "social" into every conceivable arena. Such a systematic perversion of the language had to have a purpose: to plant the thought that "social" infuses everything with a positive content. If successful, it was bound to surround the word "socialism" with a positive aura. Conspiracy? No—a well thought-out program, openly advocated and diligently implemented by its planners. They have succeeded beyond their wildest dreams. Friedrich Hayek in *The Fatal Conceit* (1988) lists over 160 nouns to which the adjective "social" has been attached with some frequency. Hayek traces the origins of the usage to German theorists and argues persuasively that "social," far from adding anything, in fact drains all nouns to which it is attached of content or meaning. Regardless, speakers of all political persuasions have taken to using the word with alarming frequency.

Why should a word, just because it became the obsession of certain German thinkers, pervade English, the language that has given us "common sense"? What would our conscience *not* prompt us to do that our "social" conscience would? Conscientious persons value life and possess a sense of duty. Conscientious persons believe in everyone's right to the pursuit of happiness, law or no. Conscience imposes an obligation to care about, and to work toward, the betterment of the human condition. What does "social" add to this list, other than a political slant?

A PROCESS OF ELIMINATION

Advocates of social justice point to the downtrodden, the dispossessed, the disenfranchised. Advocates of social justice insist that, in order to demonstrate a social conscience, a person must resolve to *eliminate* poverty, *eliminate* suffering, and *eliminate* differences among people. The assumption is that society can and will reach a state in which all its members enjoy just the right quantity and proportion of attributes, possessions, and good fortune in relation to all other members, and to their own expectations.

Special attention must be focused upon the word "eliminate." As noted, the demand to "eliminate" has been with us since the French Revolution. It is a key word, because it is peculiar to the thinking of those who advocate social justice. What are the practical implications?

In order to eliminate poverty, agreement must be reached on terminology. Poor by what standard? Poor in Albania or Zaire is very different from poor in Switzerland or the United States. Poverty, then, is relative, and in relative terms, there will always be "poverty" as long as some people have more and others have less. Two possibilities arise. One is to establish the authority which will take possession of all goods and distribute them evenly among the populace. This would have to be a continuous process because the more gifted and more industrious will keep accumulating more than the others. The second option is to concede that it is all nonsense.

The elimination of suffering presumes even greater divine powers. The worst offenders propose to eliminate suffering through various government decrees and executive orders. These same people speculate about "the elimination of differences," a truly disturbing phenomenon.

A NEW EPIDEMIC

One possible answer may be an affliction peculiar to people who apply the word "social" with great frequency. I will refer to it as "Compartmentalized Brain Syndrome," or CBS for short. Sufferers from CBS have more or less the same information as the rest of us in the various compartments of the brain. But traffic between the compartments has broken down. No connection is made between two bits of data, even within the same subject matter, such as tax rates and tax revenues. The breakdown may be either temporary or permanent.

By way of illustration, a United States senator recently complained bitterly about the diminishing interest young people show in the music of Johann Sebastian Bach. The same senator fully endorses multiculturalism. Multiculturalism is code for the gradual elimination of all Western traditions. A person who fails to recognize the connection between declaring the Western canon irrelevant, and the decline in the appreciation of Bach's music, is suffering from CBS.

The same may be said of persons who speak of "the downtrodden," "the dispossessed," and "the disenfranchised" in today's America. Clearly, no law in the United States would ever create or permit any such thing. CBS sufferers nonetheless refuse to notice that people are different, and that differences of abilities, aspirations, family circumstances, and a variety of other factors will always produce a wide range of results. Alternatively, they view people in terms of conditions that existed in times past, as if slavery or segregation were still with us, or women's suffrage not yet adopted. Persons afflicted with CBS tend to hold a number of nonsensical opinions, and nonsense cannot be justified except perhaps through more nonsense.

STATE OR PROCESS?

The ultimate nonsense is the search for social justice. This is not to insult the millions of highly respectable persons who have been deluded into adopting social justice as their goal. But the truth is, if subjected to honest scrutiny, the very concept flies in the face of both reason and experience. Worse still is the presumptuous implication that, were social justice possible, certain persons are better able than others to judge *what* it is. (Incidentally, how does such an implication square with the doctrine that we are all the same?)

"Social justice" generally means that justice must prevail in the social sphere. But society is in constant flux; its *state* undergoes constant change. Thus, if a state of justice exists in a given minute, it is unlikely to exist in the next. There will be either more or less justice. How do we monitor performance? What are the measurements? Who judges the data? And, even more troubling, what of the choice between a static and a dynamic society? Most favor a dynamic society for obvious reasons. But a dynamic society produces variable states of social justice.

According to the only theory in existence, to attain a satisfactory state of social justice, social tensions—the source of dynamism—are to be eliminated (there is that word again!). Once that is achieved, society will of course be *static*. We have to work diligently, the prescription goes, to attain a state of being with no social tensions.

The state so characterized is known as "communism."

A DISCONCERTING CONCLUSION

Unwittingly, perhaps, in many cases, but persons who advocate social justice advocate communism. Taking social justice to its logical conclusion, nothing less will suffice. The howls of protests such a conclusion is likely to elicit confirm the many misconceptions associated with the word "communism." We need to relieve the word of the misleading connotations it has acquired along the way.

That is, when we say "communism," we see the Kremlin, Soviet tanks crushing twelve-year-olds, Castro puffing on a cigar, and Mao's Red Guards cutting off the limbs of the elderly with a knife. But none of that is the essence of communism. The essence of communism is *social justice*—the elimination of poverty, the elimination of suffering, the elimination of all differences that erect walls between people. The essence of communism is the global village in which everyone benefits equally within an interdependent and socially conscious world. The essence of communism is the rearing of children by the village. Even Hitler's version, which he called "national socialism," was intended to deliver great and lasting benefits to the masses, once a few million redundant people were, well, eliminated.

We need to rid ourselves of the images of starving North Koreans, of Rumanian orphans with AIDS, of multitudes in shabby and filthy clothes, of landscapes polluted beyond recognition. That is not what communism was designed to be. That is not what communism is going to be.

Once we reach the true state of communism, we are told, there will not be poverty. There will not be suffering. There will not be differences in the living standards of people. Children will never be hungry. There will not be bonuses for corporate executives. There will no longer be some with spacious homes and others homeless. There will no longer be some who cannot afford health care and others who have elective surgery. There will not be people who are disadvantaged.

Nor will there be people who can do as they please.

There will be Social Justice.

If this does not correspond to the idea of social justice, what does? For there must be an end state, or the pursuit of "social" justice is nothing more than the excuse for a permanent state of "social"—warfare.

PRESCRIPTION FOR WAR

Warfare, of course, was precisely the vision of the person who promised us the state of perfection he called communism. His name was Karl Marx, and he was the original sufferer from CBS. His economic theory, his reading of history, his political advice to the rest of the world for the remainder of time, all show a mind seriously afflicted by that disease. How else could an otherwise brilliant mind reduce the myriad differences among people to matters of class? How else could a brilliant mind look upon the exploding kaleidoscope of history and see only class warfare? How else could a brilliant mind write the two vast volumes of *Das Kapital* based on a single arbitrary and erroneous thesis of value?

Indeed, to adopt Marx's view means to join in social warfare. The behavior of social warriors brings to mind Dostoevski's description in *Crime and Punishment* of some strange new microbes. "Men attacked by them became at once mad and furious. But never had men considered themselves so intellectual and so completely in possession of the truth as these sufferers, never had they considered their decisions, their scientific conclusions, their moral convictions so infallible...."

Social warfare clearly undermines domestic tranquility. But the even greater evil is that it fuels discontent and induces a permanent state of hopelessness by setting unattainable goals. And unattained they shall remain, except of course in communism—if you believe the theory.

Perhaps some do.

But the rest of us need to face the fact that the Rule of Law and the Search for Social Justice cannot exist side-by-side because social justice requires that those who possess more of anything have it taken away from them. The Rule of Law will not permit that. It exists to guarantee conditions in which *more* people can have *more* liberty, *more* rights, *more* possessions. Prophets of social justice—communists, whether by that or any other name focus on who should have *less*. Because they have nothing to give, they can only take away. First, they take away opportunity. Next, they take away possessions. In the end, they have to take away life itself.

Are two of the three taking hold already?

CHAPTER EIGHT

FINDING "TRUE NORTH"

LOOKING FOR DIRECTIONS

In Hungarian schools, beginning in the third grade and for several years, much attention was devoted to the matter of finding north. Teachers would go over the various methods time and time again. Living in Hungary's capital, a metropolis of considerable size, it was hard for us to imagine that we were in some imminent danger of being hopelessly lost, but we listened dutifully. We learned how to find north when the sun was out, when it was clouded over, by moonlight, using the stars, and—most importantly—when traversing a forest. The tribulations of Hansel and Gretel lived in the memory of every schoolchild, and we were anxious to find our way home even if we had no breadcrumbs to strew on the ground as we went. And so, our teachers made sure that we would never forget to look for moss on tree trunks, as moss grows invariably on the north side.

Finding "true north" is a great deal simpler for Americans. It is the Constitution of the United States, a document of remarkably few words, small enough to fit easily into a side pocket. Yet, while the Constitution is invoked by many, and often, few actually read it with any frequency and most would be surprised to find how inaccurate their references to it can be.

As we approach the new millennium, reasons abound for renewing our acquaintance with the Constitution. The "Supreme Law of our Land" survived for nearly two centuries with its validity never in doubt. But that is no longer the case. Every day, we are faced with issues that challenge the Constitution, openly or under some pretext. Indeed, for the past thirty years, a significant proportion of Americans has chosen political positions—group rights, speech codes, certain environmental regulations—no longer predicated on the Constitution. Some have done so innocently, others perniciously. And since many of our schools no longer teach the founding documents, generations have grown up, and are growing up, without the tools to evaluate respective positions in the public debate. Already a decade ago, the National Endowment for the Humanities reported a full 25 percent of college seniors unable to distinguish Winston Churchill's words from Josef Stalin's, or Karl Marx's ideas from the U.S. Constitution.

FUNDAMENTAL DIFFERENCES

When a position is taken on a specific issue, that position reflects the foundations of a person's beliefs. Notwithstanding attempts to straddle the gap by claiming to be a "fiscal conservative, social liberal," or supporting "generally smaller government but continued federal funding for education," we live in a divided country. The decisive division today is not between Democrats and Republicans, nor even between conservatives and liberals. It is between those who wish the United States of America to continue on the course which the founders charted, and those who wish to change course and see a different type of country emerge in its place.

Another way of describing this is to place on one side those who wish to live under the Rule of Law, and on the other side those who wish to search for social justice. It is safe to assume that respective positions on most issues are based on one or the other.

We have seen the history and the benefits, borne out by experience, of the Rule of Law. Does the search for social justice stand up to similar scrutiny—does it yield similarly impressive results? Since social justice presumes that certain people know best what is in the interest of certain other people, it is informative to read the comments of John Locke, in his *Essay in the Law of Nature.* "No one can be a fair and impartial judge of someone else's benefit; and you mock him by merely pretending to recognize his interest if you tell him that he can do anything that is in his interest to do, but at the same time insist that someone else should have the authority to determine what it is that is in his interest." Those who search for social justice characteristically look upon themselves as having just such authority.

Thinkers, politicians, and journalists have assembled various labels for those who have parted company with the Constitution. They are called "elitists," "statists," "utopian-collectivists," or just plain "liberals." I have added to the confusion by choosing "dogmatist" in my 1995 essay "The Battle for America's Soul." The very profusion of labels should persuade us that we have been evading the truth. Alas, any reference to "socialist," let alone "communist," is met with ridicule, and worse. And, truth be told, it is difficult to paint many ordinary, often well-meaning Americans in the same colors as our enemies. It is equally distasteful to accuse public servants of having betrayed their oath of office.

ACCEPTING REALITY

We must nevertheless free ourselves from the horrors we associate with *practical* communism (which we have seen), and, in evaluating where we stand, focus on the magnificent promise of *theoretical* communism (which, true believers say, is certain to come and will be perfect). Most believers prefer not to be called "liberals," much less "communists." Indeed, most believers in America have never thought of themselves as communists.

Yet those who advocate social justice hold, by definition, that the Constitution of the United States has failed to deliver it. Otherwise, they would simply refer to this or the other article, and insist on its faithful observance. But the original law is seen as inadequate. An avalanche of new laws, devoid of constitutional authority, has become the weapon of choice. Hiding true intent is, moreover, achieved by new, misleading rhetoric. According to this, ours is a "living, breathing Constitution."

Nothing in the arsenal of social-justice advocates can match the sinister potential lurking in that phrase.

Part of the unique success of our Constitution is its capacity to renew itself, coupled with precise provisions for the amendment process. Ensuring stability and peaceful transition of power have placed the American Constitution in a class by itself. Declaring it subject to arbitrary change—and "living, breathing" cannot mean anything else—removes its unique properties, and with them the political stability this nation has enjoyed through turmoil and strife.

Yet, how can we apply a word as strong as "communist" to people who merely advocate "flexibility" in the way the Constitution is applied, and do so in "the interest of the poor, the underprivileged, the needy, the forgotten"? Surely, this is a case of "hate speech," and just another display of "mean-spirited conservatism."

But the poor, the needy, the underprivileged, and the forgotten existed before the 1960s. Millions of them came to America from other lands, precisely because they had reason to believe that in America they would have the opportunity to improve their condition. And they were right. A constantly growing number of old and new Americans gained increasing access to the steadily accumulating wealth of the nation. The promise of liberty was fulfilled for more individuals than in any other society on earth. Until recently, no one questioned the principles on which this nation was founded,

for it was understood that adherence to these very principles produced the enviable results.

UNDERSTANDING COMMUNISM

The Rule of Law created conditions in which individuals may pursue
the best their abilities can achieve. The proponents of social justice
specify the conditions—"fair" distribution of wealth, free healthcare,
elimination of differences—society must achieve. While we are
herded from one vague and capricious campaign to the next, the theoretical description of one—and only one—state of being exists in
which all those conditions are said to have been achieved. Like it or
not, this is known by the word *communism*. If those who pride themselves on their search for social justice were honestly to face the long-
term implications, they would have to arrive at the same conclusion.

But even more important is the admission that one cannot have it
both ways. Many readers, probably a majority, will recoil at the
extensive use of the word "communism" in these pages. They might
go along with "socialism." But recall that socialism—which has gone
through a number of different definitions—is only a transitory phase
on the road to communism.

I will offer definitions of the stages leading to communism which
were used most consistently in Eastern Europe during the decades
of Soviet occupation and Communist Party rule. Of course, there,
too, the books were revised frequently, especially concerning the
history of the Bolshevik Party. But the following three phases did
not change: First, there was the "Dictatorship of the Proletariat," in
which all acts of terror were justified in order to eliminate (that word
again) the internal enemies of The People. (Enemies of The People
did not qualify as people.) Once accomplished, the building of
"Socialism" would commence, during which all would receive their
share of the national product according to individual performance at
the workplace. This, in time, would lead to "Communism" wherein

all would receive their share of the national product according to individual need.

Alas, all the "People's Democracies" (Hungary, Poland, Czechoslovakia, and East Germany) seemed forever locked in the first phase: dictatorship of the proletariat. Only the Soviet Union— "vanguard, model, hope and pride of mankind"—was in the process of building socialism. This was clear from a daily hour-long current affairs broadcast over Radio Budapest, with the title "From the Land Where Socialism is Being Built." Sometime in the early 1960s they must have completed the task, for the daily broadcast changed its title. It was now "From the Land Where Communism is Being Built." No one could recall the actual event when the Soviet Union declared that socialism had been reached, but then, who could argue?

The point is that all those who believe that socialism has merit and is intellectually acceptable, but communism is abhorrent and out of the question, are fooling themselves. It is all one package because all of it is predicated on the same way of thinking. One either signs on to the package or one does not. Partial consent is an illusion.

The package is *The Idea*, which has gone through countless transformations and as many versions. It has been "Bolshevism" in Russia, "Fascism" in Italy, "National Socialism" in Germany, "Democratic Socialism" in Sweden, and the "Long March" and "Cultural Revolution" in China. But as The Idea circled the globe, it kept finding America standing in the way. America, the impenetrable target, was on the other side. To appreciate the significance of this, we need to consider the broader context.

LONG-TERM OBJECTIVES

The battle between the two sides has raged for centuries, and it reflects as much an assertion of national identities (more on that in "Identity") as a divergence in thinking. The divergence began with Roman law and common law and deepened as economic and political organization—both extensions of legal thought—became increasingly sophisticated. But sophistication notwithstanding, the last centuries produced only two directions of basic thought. One is The Idea, a compendium of Continental European—really Franco-Germanic—theories; the other is based on Anglo-American aspirations and experience. Under a variety of labels, the former is unconcerned with human nature, and seeks only those outcomes it considers "desirable." The latter has always been engaged in creating the circumstances that, based on human nature and empirical evidence, will offer the best chances for individual success. While the latter holds that successful individuals will constitute a successful society, the former believes that a good theory will produce a "good" society—communism being the ultimate "good society."

Two world wars and a cold war (indeed a third world war) have now been fought between the two schools of thought. American victory in all three demonstrated that only with America safely in the ranks can the ultimate victory of The Idea be assured. A Communist Party of significant size never would have been possible in America. But owing to the success of a different approach (see "Property") it is no longer necessary. The Idea has been successfully installed in America's schools, as well as in most of the information and entertainment media. Academia, Hollywood, the news media, the National Education Association, and the environmental movement are far more effective than any political party. And, as high school textbooks, college courses, television newscasts, or national newspapers attest, the purpose is the *transformation* of America.

Could the advocates of "change" be after something truly new? New ideas are exceedingly rare. In reality, rather than a product of "mean spirit" or a "warm heart," everything tends to be a restatement of, or a variation on, either the Franco-Germanic or the Anglo-American line. Anything else would have to be a genuinely novel concept in the affairs of man—an unlikely prospect.

The Search for Social Justice, then, is the current Americanized version of the Franco-Germanic line—The Idea—of which communism is the end state. Unlike communism, "social justice" sounds wonderfully warm, humane, even lofty. Since social justice is pure demagoguery with no foundation in reality, it is flexible enough to enhance and camouflage anyone's personal agenda. And since conscience and responsibility for our neighbors are old American traits, it is perfect for domestic use. Accordingly, it has won over tens of millions of Americans. Most of them would not say they were liberals, much less socialists; they are simply the "caring" people. But, in the end, it all amounts to the same thing.

If we were to face that The Idea was responsible for the horrors of the twentieth century, we would realize where it is likely to take us; if we were to realize that The Idea, far from envisioning a *better* America, looks forward to *no* America, we would recoil in horror.

We would demand an immediate return to the Rule of Law.

WE STILL HAVE THE TOOLS

It is not as nebulous as it may sound. The Constitution is quite clear, and Article VI even clearer: "This Constitution, and the laws of the United States which shall be made *in Pursuance thereof*... shall be the supreme Law of the Land; and the *Judges in every State shall be bound* thereby..." [emphasis added]. Better yet, the Federalist Papers provide additional guidance.

And if the words that appear in the Constitution are clear, so too are the words that do not. Music—my home ground—consists not only of notes, but also of silences, of "rests." I will always remember the first time I heard a great teacher say, "Beethoven composed the most beautiful rests," and when I understood how to perform silence. Much in the same manner, the topics on which the Constitution is silent speak volumes about the intent of its framers. Legislators, federal agencies, and, above all, judges who fill those loud silences with their own bleating should have their public engagement canceled.

"Thou shall know the tree by its fruit," says the Bible. Indeed. The search for social justice has spawned group rights, redistribution, entitlements, and multiculturalism. None has a basis in law, none has legitimacy, but they beget one another. What is multiculturalism if not the redistribution of cultural property? What are redistribution and entitlement if not group rights? What is the rationale for group rights if not "social justice"?

By contrast, the Rule of Law has spawned rights vested solely in individuals and the guarantee of personal property—and facilitated the emergence of a common American identity. No less indispensable than the law, our common American identity has been the repository of our moral and ethical beliefs, and it has served as the guide to our practices.

RIGHTS

CHAPTER NINE

WHAT RIGHTS ARE, AND WHAT THEY ARE NOT

DEFINING RIGHTS

The rights listed in the Constitution have certain aspects in common. For our purpose here, we need only examine two of these. Individuals may assert them at will, and governments must guarantee them at all times. Our judiciary, the third branch of government, was established to interpret the scope of those rights—not to invent entirely new types and categories of them. Clearly, if we no longer agree about the nature of rights, we are challenging the very foundation of our legal order.

The apparently benevolent and compassionate tone characteristic of such challenges was well illustrated in a speech given by the Honorable Judge Stephen Reinhardt in the Ninth Circuit, U.S. Court of Appeals, to a gathering at George Washington University's School of Law in Washington, D.C., on November 12, 1996. Judge Reinhardt drew a clear distinction between conservative and liberal judges, professing to be unequivocally in the latter category. Here is an excerpt from that speech.

Liberal judges just happen to believe in good, old-fashioned American values as embodied in the Constitution, even when they are inconvenient, or lead to unpopular result. And that makes a lot of politicians uncomfortable. How can you tell a judge is a liberal? It's not that hard. Liberal judges believe in a generous or expansive interpretation of the Bill of Rights. We believe that the meaning of the Constitution was not frozen in 1789. That, as society develops and evolves, its understanding of constitutional principles also grows. We believe that the Founding Fathers used broad general principles to describe our rights, terms such as "due process of law"; "life, liberty and property"; "unreasonable search and seizure"; "freedom of speech," because they were determined not to erect, enact a narrow, rigid code that would bind and limit all future generations. Many of the rights Americans cherish the most are not among those listed in the Constitution. For example, the right to marry; the right to have children, as many or as few as one wants; and even the right to travel.

A "LIVING, BREATHING" CONSTITUTION?

In the previous chapter, we encountered what is called the "living, breathing" Constitution. That is precisely what Judge Reinhardt's "generous or expansive interpretation of the Bill of Rights" means. That is the message hidden in the phrases, "We believe that the meaning of the Constitution was not frozen in 1789," and "As society develops and evolves, its understanding of constitutional principles also grows." Alas, society does not have an understanding; individual judges do.

The U.S. Constitution may reflect "good, old-fashioned American values," but what it embodies is a set of *laws*. As clearly stated in Article VI, the Constitution is "the supreme law of the Land," by which the "Judges in every State shall be bound." Judges take an oath upon the Constitution, and the language contains no reference to "society's evolving understanding." Values may influence the drafting of laws, and values may also influence their interpretation. But the function of the Constitution is to provide a framework in which the alteration of any one component is possible only through the assent of an overwhelming majority.

What do we make of the assertion by a highly placed member of the judiciary that "rights not listed in the Constitution are cherished, if anything, more than the ones that are"? What is the source of such rights? Who guarantees them? Judge Reinhardt's first example is the right to marry. But since marriage will occur only with the *consent* of two people, no individual can assert a right to it. Government cannot require the consent of either party, thus government cannot deliver a guarantee for it.

And what of "the right to have children, as many or as few as one wants"? A right cannot depend on biological prerequisites beyond our control. No government can guarantee that a man and a woman both will possess the cells necessary to combine, that they shall combine as many times as the man and the woman jointly desire, and that nothing will interfere with the delicate process of carrying the embryo to full term for a live birth—all provisions and processes beyond the power and control of man.

"The right to travel," a key provision of the Magna Carta, falls into a different category. By the time the Bill of Rights was written, the right to move about had been in existence for nearly six centuries. It did not require restatement and, in any event, is covered by the Ninth Amendment: "The enumeration in the Constitution, of certain rights, shall not be construed to deny or disparage others retained by the people." It is important to keep in mind that the wording refers to rights, and not to judicial opinions.

The act of changing locations does qualify as a right: It may be asserted by an individual, and it is capable of being guaranteed by government. Neither marriage nor having children falls into the same category. Listing them together is an attempt to obscure important differences, and it amounts to treatment of the Constitution that is best described as a smorgasbord approach. This is the case when judges take from the Constitution what satisfies their appetite at the moment and ignore the rest, or when they replace certain items as the occasion arises. The Ninth Amendment is not a blanket authority to create new rights at will.

On the other hand, the precise wording of the Ninth Amendment demonstrates an important aspect of our Constitution, present also in many other articles. It is the *presumption* of rights, as opposed to the *grant* of rights. The operative phrases are "The right of the people shall not be abridged" (or violated), or: "Congress shall make no law...." On the one hand, the people have those rights in the first place; they are not granted them by government. On the other, our laws were designed to place the restrictions on the possessors of power—not on defenseless individuals.

BOGUS RIGHTS

The consequences of what Judge Reinhardt describes as a "generous or expansive" interpretation of the Constitution can be found on the Internet. Under "Politics & Law>Rights Issues," the search engine *Excite* offers the following list: *2nd Amendment; Abortion; Animal Rights; Censorship; Children's Rights; Civil Rights; Disabled; Environmental Rights; Gender Rights; Helmets for Cyclists; Homeless; Human Rights; Religious Rights; Smokers & Nonsmokers*. A special review is offered about SCSAC, the coalition "championing the rights of the larger-than-average citizen," and I personally witnessed the campaign in Florida to assert the *rights of LEPs* ("Persons with Limited English Proficiency") to enroll into a professional drama school.

With the exception of the "2nd Amendment" and "Censorship" (which presumably deals with First Amendment rights), none of the above is a right. We may chuckle at the mention of rights for "larger-than-average citizens," but we are very serious indeed about "human rights"—not to mention "civil rights."

The term "civil rights" is permanently attached to the movement that finally won full equality for black Americans. As such, it will survive as long as American history continues. Yet as a category of rights, the term "civil rights" does not exist. The same pertains to "human rights"—a term applied to countries and regions in which the concept of rights exists scarcely, if at all. "Human" rights? What other rights are there?

And that, very quickly, brings us to the point—the need for precision. If there are "human" rights, there can also be animal "rights." If there are "civil" rights, we can also have children's, women's, and gay-lesbian "rights." And many claim that we do.

But the only *legitimate* rights available to citizens of the United States are those anchored in the Constitution, and available to all. Women, children, homosexuals, blacks, and people with multiple chemical reactivity do not have additional rights. What or who would be the authority for such rights?

The "rights" nonsense, now enveloping society like a giant spider's web, began with a most honorable premise. Because certain people, occasionally or consistently, were deprived of the full benefits that flow from our constitutional rights, movements sprang up to secure these benefits for all. For easy identification, each movement adopted a label, such as "women's rights." It stands to reason that a rally staged by the "Organization-to-Ensure-that-No-Woman-is-Denied-a-Right-Traditionally-Available-to-Members-of-the-Opposite-Sex" would be cumbersome to advertise. "Women's rights" is concise, catchy. The tragedy occurred when the leaders of all such movements realized that their power and livelihood would disappear as soon as society made the necessary adjustment. And so, the "rights" battle continued in complicity with judges who are confused about the law, as witness Mr. Reinhardt. And since the creation of a group must precede the demand for rights, more and more groups have been created. The rationale is that the more people belong to one group or another, the greater the assurance that "group rights" would be here to stay. The incentive for belonging to a group is the visible success of groups in securing additional "rights," and so the vicious cycle is perpetuated.

GROUPS

Groups are as impossible to define as "social justice." The first question must be: Is everyone a member of a group? If not, how can equality be promoted when some people are in a group, and others are not? If all people are in one group or another, is everyone a member of only one group, or is membership open to a person in any number of different groups? Is there a limit on the number of groups in which a person may be a member for official purposes? And *who decides* all these questions?

This may sound facetious, but it is deadly serious business. People are punished if they fail to take it seriously. If the questions do not demonstrate the nonsensical nature of the proposition, attempts to answer them will.

Take, for example, a black teenage girl who walks with a limp and is being brought up by lesbians. Is she a child? Is she a woman? Is she an African-American? Is she disabled? Is she a lesbian? She must know, because the government wants to know. If she answers yes to all the questions, she will have herself a whole basketful of rights. Over and above her constitutional rights, she possesses children's rights (still), women's rights (already), affirmative action rights, disabled rights, and gay-lesbian rights. People have to be mindful of speaking not only *to* her, but *about* her. Anyone near her is but one step away from sensitivity training at best, loss of livelihood at worst.

Once again, the more groups we have, the more "rights" we have. The more groups we have, the farther we drift from the rule of law.

The more groups we have, the more restrictions we have on our true rights: individual rights.

Individual rights reflect our similarities; group rights emphasize our differences. Individual rights promote equality; group rights cultivate inequality. Individual rights permit every one of us to be special; group rights create stereotypes. Individual rights are unalienable, and are guaranteed by the Constitution; group rights are born at activist rallies, conferred by a party-political executive branch, and confirmed by a temporal judge. Group rights can be taken away by an even louder rally, a different regulator, a new judge.

Individual rights and group rights are mutually exclusive; we cannot have it both ways.

Individual rights provide a sense of security. The greater the sense of security, the more of people's creativity will be converted to productivity. The higher the productivity, the greater the sense of independence.

Group rights instill fear. The greater the fear, the more the limitations on human activity. The greater the limitations, the more total the dependency on the wielders of regulatory power.

Group rights—invented rights, that is—come, of course, with an important financial dimension. The bearer is entitled to unearned benefits—more directly put, to the fruits of other people's labor. Of greater significance, however, is the gradual destruction of society by the fear that attends group rights.

WHEN A GROUP IS NOT A "GROUP"

A discussion of group rights must consider various forms of association for which legal provisions exist. "What about corporations? What about farmers?" are popular retorts to assertions that group rights lack legitimacy.

The act of forming, joining, or leaving corporations is freely available to all. They are based on the right to free association, and the right freely to enter into contract between consenting parties. If the freely elected representatives of the people deem it in the public interest to establish certain rights for corporations, such rights are available to all, since anyone may form or join a corporation—or leave one, as the case may be. Anyone may become a farmer, or decide no longer to be one.

By contrast, "women's rights," "children's rights," and "affirmative action rights" pertain to persons who have no choice in the matter. An individual is neither in a position to become a member by choice, nor—by an act of will—to give up membership in the group. Either through the accident of birth, or by Directive No. 15 of the Office of Management and Budget—which governs racial and ethnic classifications—persons are locked in for life.

"Locked in for life"—surely nothing stands in greater contradiction to the very foundations of this country. People have been coming here for more than two centuries in an effort to escape the constraints of birth that stood in the way of the pursuit of happiness in their native lands. The very essence of America has been unrestricted mobility—up, down, or sideways—in the societal structure. And, yes, "down" has been important, too. In societies of privilege, a safety net exists for the privileged, so that no penalty is accrued for lack of industry, bad habits, or irresponsible lifestyles. Such a safety net is bound to erode the dynamic properties of any society. But the worst feature of group rights is that they symbolize and perpetuate man's inability to escape the constraints of birth—an echo of Lenin, Hitler, and Stalin. "A Jew is always a Jew," said Hitler. "A bourgeois is always a bourgeois," said Lenin and Stalin.

Finally, corporate-type rights are quite different from constitutional rights. Congress (or any of the several states) can grant rights to corporations and other forms of associations, but the same body can also alter or remove such rights.

By contrast, the fundamental individual rights guaranteed in the Constitution are not "subject to change" by any legislative body on its own; they require an amendment of the Constitution. The purveyors of group rights demand that same elevated status for their special benefit, but without going through the constitutional process. Of course, they realize that the constitutional process would deliver a resounding "No" to every one of these demands.

So, when is a right not a right? When it is neither possible for an individual to assert it, nor for government to guarantee it, and—last but not least—when it is not equally available to all citizens.

A footnote to government guarantees, especially for readers who might have fallen victim to the outrageous suggestions that food, shelter, and health care are among the "rights" of people. The legitimate means for government to guarantee rights are confined to the provision of legal remedies, enforcement, and the maintenance of public order. The confiscation of property, such as a portion of one's income, for the purpose of satisfying claims which originate in group rights lacks legitimacy to the same extent as the group rights themselves (see "Property").

This chapter explored rights which are *not*. It also places in sharper focus those rights which really, unalienably, *are*.

TEN COMMANDMENTS—
TEN AMENDMENTS

CONSTRAINTS AND LIBERTIES

One need not be a practitioner of any religion to appreciate the enormous significance that the Ten Commandments had in America's founding, regardless of their origin. Of course, although the reader may not, the founders did believe in their divine origin. And, whenever in the long path of history the Ten Commandments emerged, their implications for what became known as the civilized world cannot be overstated.

In the broadest sense, we might think of man's existence in three phases. The first was characterized by the unbridled freedom of instinctive behavior, much as in the animal world. The second brought constraints which, for some time, were forced upon the many by the few. Third, and closer to our own time, the ability of some to recognize the benefits that result from an acceptance of constraints led to the emergence of liberties within a well-defined structure. As acceptance of the constraints broadened, the guarantee of liberties could be extended. The most notable success of this reciprocal relationship may be observed in two centuries of immigration to America. Until recently, the premise has been a simple one:

Newcomers who were willing to accept the constraints, not necessarily extant in their country of origin, were offered a share in the liberties. Chief among these has been the recognition that the only dependable guarantee of one's own rights is the concession and guarantee of those same rights to one's neighbor.

In Chapter 4, we traced the origins of equality before the law to King Arthur and the Magna Carta. In a sense, the origins go back as far as the Ten Commandments, which are the same for the powerful and for the humble. Numerous direct threads lead from certain commandments to the Bill of Rights, making the connection even more tangible.

For easy reference, we reproduce the text of the Ten Commandments as well as the first ten amendments to the U.S. Constitution, known as the Bill of Rights.

THE TEN COMMANDMENTS

And God spake all these words, saying,

(1)   I am the Lord thy God, which have brought thee out of the land of Egypt, out of the house of bondage. Thou shalt have no other gods before me.

(2)   Thou shalt not make unto thee any graven image, or any likeness of any thing that is in heaven above, or that is in the earth beneath, or that is in the water under the earth:

Thou shalt not bow down thyself to them, nor serve them: for I the Lord thy God am a jealous God, visiting the iniquity of the fathers upon the children unto the third and fourth generation of them that hate me;

And showing mercy unto thousands of them that love me, and keep my commandments.

(3) Thou shalt not take the name of the Lord thy God in vain; for the Lord will not hold him guiltless that taketh his name in vain.

(4) Remember the Sabbath day, to keep it holy. Six days shalt thou labor, and do all thy work: But the seventh day is the Sabbath of the Lord thy God: in it thou shalt not do any work, thou, nor thy son, nor thy daughter, thy manservant, nor thy maidservant, nor thy cattle, nor thy stranger that is within thy gates: For in six days the Lord made heaven and earth, the sea, and all that in them is, and rested the seventh day: wherefore the Lord blest the sabbath day, and hallowed it.

(5) Honor thy father and thy mother: that thy days may be long upon the land which the Lord thy God giveth thee.

(6) Thou shalt not kill.

(7) Thou shalt not commit adultery.

(8) Thou shalt not steal.

(9) Thou shalt not bear false witness against thy neighbor.

(10) Thou shalt not covet thy neighbor's house, thou shalt not covet thy neighbor's wife, nor his manservant, nor his maidservant, nor his ox, nor his ass, nor any thing that is thy neighbor's.

THE FIRST TEN AMENDMENTS
TO THE CONSTITUTION

ARTICLE I

Congress shall make no law respecting an establishment of religion, or prohibiting the free exercise thereof; or abridging the freedom of speech, or of the press; or the right of the people peaceably to assemble, and to petition the Government for a redress of grievances.

ARTICLE II

A well-regulated Militia, being necessary to the security of a free State, the right of the people to keep and bear Arms shall not be infringed.

ARTICLE III

No Soldier shall, in time of peace be quartered in any house, without the consent of the Owner, nor in time of war, but in a manner to be prescribed by law.

ARTICLE IV

The right of the people to be secure in their persons, houses, papers, and effects, against unreasonable searches and seizures, shall not be violated, and no Warrants shall issue, but upon probable cause, supported by Oath or affirmation, and particularly describing the place to be searched, and the persons or things to be seized.

ARTICLE V

No person shall be held to answer for a capital or otherwise infamous crime, unless on a presentment or indictment of a Grand Jury, except in cases arising in the land or naval forces, or in the Militia, when in actual service in time of War or public danger; nor shall any person be subject for the same offence to be twice put in jeopardy of life or limb; nor shall be compelled in any criminal case to be a witness against himself, nor be deprived of life, liberty, or property, without due process of law; nor shall private property be taken for public use, without just compensation.

Article VI

In all criminal prosecutions, the accused shall enjoy the right to a speedy and public trial, by an impartial jury of the State and district wherein the crime shall have been committed, which district shall have been previously ascertained by law, and to be informed of the nature and cause of the accusation; to be confronted with the witnesses against him; to have compulsory process for obtaining witnesses in his favor, and to have the Assistance of Counsel for his defense.

Article VII

In Suits at common law, where the value in controversy shall exceed twenty dollars, the right of a trial by jury shall be preserved, and no fact tried by a jury shall be otherwise re-examined in any Court of the United States, than according to the rules of the common law.

Article VIII

Excessive bail shall not be required, nor excessive fines imposed, nor cruel and unusual punishments inflicted.

Article IX

The enumeration in the Constitution, of certain rights, shall not be construed to deny or disparage others retained by the people.

Article X

The powers not delegated to the United States by the Constitution, nor prohibited by it to the States, are reserved to the States respectively, or to the people.

CONNECTIONS

Articles I and X may be traced directly to the First Commandment, for rulers and governments not bound by such constraints tend to claim divine rights over their subjects. Articles IV and VI harken back to the Ninth Commandment. The Sixth, Eighth and Tenth Commandments are all at work in Articles III and V.

But the latent connections are more important still. Only a society in which the great majority will, as a matter of voluntary choice, refrain from killing can successfully operate a government by the consent of the governed. Only a society in which the great majority shall, as a matter of voluntary choice, refrain from stealing can depend on adjudication by a jury of peers. Only a society in which the great majority will curb its desire to covet a neighbor's house or a neighbor's wife can do away with "cruel and unusual" punishments, still much in use in most parts of the world.

The Fifth Commandment, positioned after the relationship with the Creator had been defined, and before the prohibitions of the Second Tablet, sets up nothing less than the prerequisites for the development of traditions. People wonder why respect for one's parents would lead to a longer life on earth. Yet the message becomes clear if we substitute society for the individual. Only through respecting the people and events upon whose shoulders each generation stands can the longevity of a *society* be secured (see "Identity"). Worth noting: The wording of the Fifth Commandment, placing equal emphasis on "father" and "mother," demonstrates that the equal importance of men and women was recognized some time before the suffragette movement.

The ascent from the animal stage proceeded with a quantum leap when the need for constraints was first recognized, articulated, and accepted. The eventual broad acceptance of constraints, moreover, made it possible to build a functioning society on liberties as expressed through individual rights (as opposed to instances in history when liberties were, and remained, mere slogans). But what happens when the rights are asserted, while the constraints are no longer accepted? The question is relevant, for such, indeed, is the prevailing attitude in the America of the 1990s.

RIGHTS WITHOUT CONSTRAINTS

Freedom of speech is no longer paired with the obligation to respect anything or anyone, not even the implied obligation to be informed about the topic. Freedom of the press no longer demands observation of the Ninth Commandment: "Thou shalt not bear false witness...." People can no longer effectively petition the government by voting for a proposition, for government has abandoned the Second Commandment and made its party-political agenda the god to which it "bows down."

Yet the area most revealing is the changing behavior of men and women. Other than eating, procreation is where our behavior most resembles the animal world, except that humans can procreate the year round. This, and the formation of societies, required that protocols be adopted for appropriate sexual activity to temper the ever-present urge, and to secure a protective environment for children.

But recently, one-by-one, these constraints have been abandoned, even ridiculed. It is packaged, of course, as an act of liberation, but in truth it leads back to animal behavior—a comment that may be unfair to animals.

While few would want to see a return of the attitudes that could ruin the college career of a female student because someone reported her for dancing to gramophone records in a boy's apartment (an incident I remember from my college days in Florida), the foregoing discussion is a poignant example of the general trend—rights without constraints.

The constant invention of new "rights" is a creature of similar pedigree. The Constitution was designed to act as a constraint upon rights subsequently demanded of, or considered by, future lawmakers. The Constitution was designed to act as a constraint upon judges who would exceed their authority. The Constitution was designed to act as a constraint upon an executive branch that substituted divine prerogative for a simple discharge of its duties.

And here we see how the search for equality before the law connects the legend of King Arthur's Round Table to the Ten Commandments; how the Rule of Law operates as much through constraints as through individual rights; how the founders of America sought out the noblest and most successful "fathers" and "mothers" of man's past and, by respecting them in the true sense of the Fifth Commandment, ensured that the nation thus created might enjoy "long days upon the land...."

THE FRAGILE EQUILIBRIUM

To what extent, then, are our rights "unalienable"? Are they ours outright, or do they come with strings attached?

Attention to the wording in the Declaration of Independence soon dispels any misconceptions. "We hold these truths to be self-evident, that all men are created equal, that they are endowed by their Creator with certain unalienable Rights, that among these are Life, Liberty and the pursuit of Happiness." The statement traces the origin of these "Rights" to the same Creator who is author of the constraints articulated in the Ten Commandments. One avails oneself of both—or neither.

The rights enumerated in the Constitution are ours to assert. The powers granted in the Constitution are for government to exercise. The rights are individual, the powers are limited. Whereas the Ninth Amendment acknowledges the potential existence of *rights* not enumerated in the Constitution, government cannot claim *powers* about which the Constitution is silent.

The first conclusion, then, is that government loses its legitimacy as soon as it exercises powers not granted to it in the Supreme Law of the Land. But the conclusions to be drawn by *the people* are no less important. Over and above the actual wording, the unbreakable relationship between rights and constraints provides the rationale for rights to be vested exclusively in individuals. *Only an individual is capable of exercising rights in full recognition and acceptance of the accompanying constraints.* Groups as such are not responsible, and the law has no means by which to hold them accountable.

Individual accountability functions also as the foundation of government by the consent of the governed. The counterpart of the irresponsible citizen is the unaccountable, faceless bureaucrat. Together, they destroy the delicate equilibrium that has taken thousands of years to achieve, and then only for the lucky few. As always, that which has taken millennia to build can be destroyed in the blink of an eye. The forces that bring about destruction of the delicate equilibrium are hard at work in our midst. While it is next to impossible to comprehend their motivation, the methods they employ are there for all to see.

CHAPTER ELEVEN

OF CLASS WARS
AND GROUP WARS

THE NEED TO KNOW

The United States of America is supposed to function as a country in which 250 million plus individuals lead the life they desire, at once facilitated and confined by law, tradition, and civilized consideration. Government is supposed to perform the functions clearly indicated by the opening paragraphs of the Declaration of Independence and the Preamble to the Constitution.

Instead, we have come to accept forced existence as members in various groups that are at odds with one another. Government, in this convoluted state, has become the indispensable arbiter of fortunes. With one hand, it eggs on the various groups, implying that they are entitled to more. With the other hand, it dispenses favors to groups that constantly stand in line, vying to be the next recipient.

It is a vicious cycle with no end in sight, ensuring a permanent state of war—the exact opposite of the "domestic tranquility" the founders sought to "insure."

If the concept of group warfare did not originate in the American Founding, where did it? *All who are aware that this was not the intended way for our nation to function must ask themselves this question.*

To date the only type of societal organization whose detailed description claims that social justice—the professed goal of group rights and group warfare—will have been achieved is communism. If that is the case, group warfare is likely to be a prescription of those who believe that communism is the ideal state for humans.

THE FRENCH CONNECTION

In order to trace the origins—and the curriculum—we must go back at least as far as the eighteenth century when political thinking in France laid the foundations for the monumental fiasco known as the French Revolution of 1789. In the same number of years it had taken America to travel the road from the Declaration of Independence to the signing of the Constitution (1776–1787), the French went from beheading their king to the coronation of their new emperor (1793–1804). The mindless slaughter that filled the gap was the translation of French political philosophy into practice.

It is important to evaluate deeds, as opposed to words. Irreversible decline threatens America today because tens of millions of our citizens are making political decisions based on words they hear, as opposed to deeds they experience. French political thought and its successor, German political thought, have brought forth libraries full of words, and still do. The words are emotive; the words are intoxicating; the words are powerful to the point where they make people ignore, overlook, and forget the deeds.

The words of the French Enlightenment affected people in ways that no set of ideas had, perhaps, since the Bible. The names Diderot, Montesquieu, Voltaire, and Rousseau are forever enshrined in the minds of educated people. The twenty-eight volumes of Diderot's *Encyclopédie* became the new model for the systematized presentation of knowledge and thought. To Montesquieu we owe the articulation of separated powers in government. Voltaire, many still believe, was endowed with the clearest and most incisive mind of the age; and few remained unmoved by the power of Rousseau's pen.

Montesquieu derived his advocacy of the separation of powers from the British model. Voltaire unequivocally admired John Locke and Isaac Newton, attributing British successes to the freedom of political discussion and to the use of reason to evaluate empirical evidence. But it was Rousseau's *Social Contract* and his judgment of man as "corrupted and rotten to the core by society and its institutions" that came to dominate French prescriptions for the future.

Voltaire had the good fortune of being exiled to Britain, where he came to understand the paths to success. When Rousseau sent him a copy of his *Social Contract*, Voltaire acknowledged it as follows:

> I have received your new book against the human race, and I thank you for it. Never was such cleverness used in the design of making us all stupid. One longs, in reading your book, to walk on all fours. But as I have lost that habit more than sixty years ago, I feel unhappily the impossibility of resuming it.

Voltaire's response is as valid today as then. Rousseau's errors, and the damage inflicted upon humanity by them, are as potent today as then. Brilliant as Rousseau was, he failed to understand that one ought not to demolish without immediately reconstructing; one ought not disseminate ideas which have no foundation in the human experience. But then, that was precisely the difference between the French Descartes and the English Locke, as Voltaire noted. The former advocated the application of reason *before*; the latter, *after* the event.

Apart from an unparalleled self-importance, Rousseau's fatal mistake was the proposition that man was in need of, and capable of, perfecting, which was exacerbated by his emotive dismissal of institutions. Once man's need and ability to be perfected are espoused, the way is clear for those who "know just how to do it"—which is

why the Anglo-Scottish approach always focused on the improvement of conditions and *institutions*, rather than of man. If, as
Rousseau suggests, institutions, in and of themselves, are corrupting, their role has been permanently undermined.

And that is why the French Revolution of 1789 failed to accomplish a positive goal: it did not have one. It merely sought to demolish the existing. Man was still "in need of perfecting"; societal
institutions were still the "source of corruption." Unsurprisingly, a
cacophony of ideas, agendas, events, and power brokers erupted.
Consequently, it became a matter of transitory opinion whose head
ought to be chopped off by the guillotine, and control of the executioner elevated the controller to being the "next hope of the people."
Danton countenanced the massacres until he was beheaded on orders
of Robespierre, and Robespierre was himself beheaded a few months
later. In the absence of workable institutions, it was only a matter of
time before a supreme ruler would have to restore order and govern
France once again. Bonaparte crowned himself emperor in 1804.

Even more decisive for posterity, however, was the spectacle of
mass executions in an effort to eliminate entire categories of people—clergy, royalists, aristocrats. The unprecedented bloodbath
conjured up new ways of manipulating history. Marx was the first to
recognize its unlimited potential. Lenin, Stalin, Hitler, Mao, and Pol
Pot showed the world how it could be done on a truly massive scale.

MEANWHILE IN AMERICA

Deeds notwithstanding, misconceptions abound with regard to what
some see as a profound influence of the French Revolution on the
American Founding. These notions are entirely unfounded for
more than one reason.

First is the matter of chronology. The French Revolution began,
officially, with the storming of the Bastille on July 14, 1789. By that
time, George Washington had already been sworn in as our first

president. The Constitution of the United States had been in effect for more than a year. Alexander Hamilton, James Madison, and John Jay had completed the essays known as the Federalist Papers before Egality! Fraternity! Liberty! were first proclaimed in Paris.

But the more important reasons have to do with intent and, perhaps, temperament. In France, the old regime had to be discarded. A profusion of ideas was in the air, but no tangible, viable concept for the organization of a new regime. The unavoidable consequence was a power struggle among groups, each proposing ideas, as opposed to principles and corresponding means for a framework of government. The number of failed experiments at organizing society would read like a farce, were it not for the scores of people killed in the process. The operative purpose of the vying groups was simply to seize power. There were the Girondins and the Jacobins, the First Republic and the Second Republic, the Committee and the Directory, the Second Directory and Thermidor, and—yes—The Consulate.

On the other side of the Atlantic, the signers of America's Declaration of Independence proclaimed their quarrel with the "present King of England," not with the existing system of laws. Indeed, the king stood accused of abandoning "the free system of English laws" and of refusing "his Assent to Laws, the most wholesome and necessary for the public good." The measured sobriety of the Declaration, even at a moment of the most intense emotions, is in stark contrast to the recurring outbursts, the slogan-oriented demagoguery that characterized events in France.

One reason for the difference between events in France and in America may be found in the calmer temperament of Englishmen. But more to the point is their early recognition of the unquestionable link that binds the concepts of law, property, and freedom. And so, for the French, liberty was something to proclaim from the rooftops; for the British, it was a state to be achieved as the result of understanding human nature, of adopting solid principles, of creating a lasting system of laws and institutions.

America's founders were, of course, intimately acquainted with the ideas of the French Enlightenment. Benjamin Franklin and Thomas Jefferson had spent time in Paris during the critical years directly preceding the French Revolution, and all were voracious readers. But although the Bill of Rights is thought to reflect the French Declaration of the Rights of Man and the Citizen, it was really the other way around. The origin of the rights enumerated in the first ten amendments is to be found in the Magna Carta, the English Bill of Rights of 1689 ("Act declaring the Rights and Liberties of the Subject and Setleing [sic] the Succession of the Crowne"), and Virginia's 1776 Declaration of Rights, drafted chiefly by George Mason. Nothing in the French approach resembles Madison's wording, which frames most rights in terms of *constraints upon government.*

Despite French prominence in the "Age of Reason," the events as they unfolded in France were determined by the rule of emotion. In America, the choice was determined by study, experience, and contemplation.

The French aimed to eliminate—the old order, the ruling class, the church. Americans, as soon as independence permitted, endeavored to build a society that would embody the noblest, time-tested, most successful principles known to man.

The French proceeded to export their ideas through conquest. Americans made their achievement available by inviting the people of the world to come and participate.

It was in France—not in America—that a giant experiment began, and continues in our time. America was established almost instantaneously—not as an experiment, but as a nation.

BRITAIN AND FRANCE—THE ORIGINAL SPLIT

Long before the end of the eighteenth century, fundamental differences emerged between French and British political thought. By

way of illustrating a philosophy of extremes: From Descartes derives
the belief in the unlimited power of reason; from Rousseau the
utterly impractical concept of a "return to nature," as well as a love
for mankind in the abstract under which lurks a tangible distaste for
people of flesh and blood. Opposite to this stands John Locke's
unceremonious acceptance of man's limitations and sober search for
what is attainable in the real world. Locke understood that institutions will corrupt man only so long as their powers are all-pervasive.
If their powers are limited, institutions—such as government—will
function in the service of the individual. And respect for the individual was viewed as the only viable basis for human relations. In addition, unlike their French (and, later, German) counterparts, British
thinkers did not see the need to challenge or supplant God.

"The tree shall be known by its fruit." The end of the eighteenth
century furnished British political thought with its greatest triumph:
the establishment of the United States of America. The same period
saw French ideas degenerating into a circular group and class warfare.

GERMANS TAKE OVER

Enter fresh troops. Throughout the eighteenth century, German
writers, philosophers, and writer-philosophers had been gathering to
assume their place, center stage. The time had now come to take note
of the breathtaking lineup: Leibniz, Kant, Hegel, and Schopenhauer;
Lessing, Goethe, Schiller, and Humboldt—just for openers.

In the same year Americans were signing their Constitution,
Immanuel Kant published the second, improved edition of his
epoch-making work: *Critique of Pure Reason*. But it is in the Preface
to the First Edition (1781) that Kant makes his motives clear. One
was to take up the argument with John Locke and rescue "pure" reason from the "dangers" of reasoning based on experience; the other,
to serve notice of human reason's ability to be infallible. "I decided
on this only course and, in doing so, flatter myself in having avoided

all those errors which hitherto have set reason at variance with itself." In other words, the work that follows would be free from error. Before Kant, infallibility had been reserved for God. It would take another hundred years before Nietzsche declared God "dead," but Kant lays the groundwork. As the German poet and philosopher Heinrich Heine later (1833) commented: "Kant is the Robespierre of philosophy; the executioner of God."

The seizure by Germans of the torch hitherto carried by French thinkers was to have momentous effects. In certain ways, German intellect is in a class by itself. There is a uniquely German obsession to seek all-encompassing answers to all questions, a German belief that such answers are there to be found, and a German ability to create systems in philosophy—and in everything else. To these talents we owe such gifts to mankind as Bach's *The Art of the Fugue*; Goethe's *Faust*; Beethoven's Ninth Symphony; Humboldt's singular grasp of the world; and Wagner's *Die Meistersinger von Nürnberg*. But in the field of philosophy, what began as an exceptionally distinguished line of thinkers turned, increasingly, into an endless succession of men who instructed the rest of us about the ways we ought to understand and "improve" ourselves and those around us. Notwithstanding the continued presence of French socialists, syndicalists, and (later) existentialists, France, from this moment onward, becomes a sideshow.

It was nonetheless through the accident of a French essay, *The Philosophy of Misery* by Pierre Joseph Proudhon, that the world first heard from Karl Marx who wrote a rebuttal under the title, *The Misery of Philosophy*. That pun may have been Marx's only exhibition of humor. He was equally devoid of the humility of Bach, the wisdom of Goethe, the humanity of Beethoven, and the ardor of Humboldt. He is said to have learned dialectics from Friedrich Hegel and materialism from Ludwig Feuerbach, but it is the obtuseness of their prose that comes through above all. Marx's contempt for people rivals that of Rousseau; his arrogance is without precedent.

It was fashionable in both the eighteenth and nineteenth centuries to interpret the past and analyze the present. Marx took it upon himself not only to define past and present, but also to prescribe the future with breathtaking assurance. Above it all, he declared his theories to be "science." Marx began Chapter One of his *Communist Manifesto* with nothing less than a "final" pronouncement about history: "The history of all hitherto existing society is the history of class struggle." (It might be easier to dismiss this obviously myopic idea, were it not the basis of today's so-called *National Standards of History* which is determining the teaching of history in America.) John Plamenatz, fellow of Nuffield College, Oxford, setting aside his usually dispassionate style, describes what ought to make Marxian social theory alien to British and American sensibilities:

> It is... demanding, arrogant, and contemptuous; it thrusts aside with disdain whatever does not suit it, as if facts were not worth noticing unless they bore it out. It is a German theory, overwhelming in its profuseness, like a broad river in full spate carrying everything before it.... There is a power often uncontrolled by reason in the roar and clatter of the long German sentences as they make their heavy way regardless of obstacles, irresistibly towards the 'Truth'....

THE NEW RELIGION

With the arrival of Marx, what had clearly become Franco-Germanic political philosophy served notice that it intended to be nothing less than a new religion. Among other things, it advocated replacing Christian concepts of an abstract struggle between Good and Evil with a most tangible struggle between groups who would henceforth be defined as "good" or "evil." The proletariat was "good," capitalists were "evil"; farmhands were good, kulaks were evil; Aryans were good, Jews were evil. Not even the possibility of individual redemption was left open in this punitive world. There was no escape from the group. Once a capitalist, always a capitalist. Once a Jew, always a Jew. (Once a white male, always a white male.)

Marx's most outstanding pupils, Vladimir Ilyich Lenin and Adolf Hitler, chose from the Master's repertoire according to their personal preference, while remaining mindful of local conditions. Lenin chose class, Hitler chose race. Both were crude, and both killed millions in the process. For long-term results, for effective rule over the *living*, a higher degree of sophistication needed to be developed. In any event, Lenin had already tried—and failed—to win Americans over to the idea of traditional class war. In 1918 he dispatched a letter to Americans about "the depth of the abyss which divides a handful of brazen billionaires who are wallowing in dirt and in luxury on the one hand, and millions of toilers who are always on the verge of starvation.... The American billionaires... have plundered hundreds of billions of dollars. And every dollar is stained with filth... and every dollar is stained with blood...." Apart from the "elegance" of Lenin's prose, it seemed unlikely that orthodox class warfare would work in a society where Henry Ford put so many behind the wheel of a Model T, and where the majority owned the roof over their heads.

THE ASSAULT ON AMERICA

The next opportunity came in 1936, when disinformation about the Spanish Civil War sent prominent Americans to fill the ranks of the North American Committee to Aid Spanish Democracy—an outfit invented, organized, and controlled by the Communist International. But credit for the jackpot must go to Josef Stalin. To begin with, he attached the label "fascist" to the Third Reich, thereby covering up the socialist nature—and name—of the ruling party, the National Socialist German Workers' Party, which sported a completely socialist agenda. Next, he used the German attack on the Soviet Union to disseminate the myth that communism was "anti-fascist," covering up not only years of nazi war exercises on hospitable Soviet soil, but the Hitler-Stalin pact of 1938 as well.

The growing segment of Americans that viewed nazism, naturally, as "evil" was now ready to regard communism as "good." Americans were utterly confused by Stalin's sleight of hand, forever persuaded that, whatever the "transitory" problems, socialism (communism) must be basically good because it fought the nazis. That "Nazi" was short for National *Socialist*, and that it proved socialism to be the same whatever the qualifying word, escaped—and continues to escape—the attention of most. That "social justice" was as much Hitler's slogan as it is today the battle cry of American liberals, has been long forgotten.

Even so, a number of special circumstances needed to come together before Americans could be induced to forget their sober, healthy, successful principles, and submit to the cunning, the evil, and the nightmare of group warfare.

CHAPTER TWELVE

TARGET: AMERICA

TWO VIEWS OF THE WORLD

Awareness of the long-term rivalry between the two lines of thought makes sense of much in history, and even more of contemporary developments. The designations "Franco-Germanic" and "Anglo-American" were chosen because they are broadly accurate, and because they make it clear that the conflict is not between different interpretations of American principles. The designations pertain only to political philosophy and its fruits. Obviously, the contributions to mankind of France and Germany as cultures, of French and German individuals, are at the top of any list.

It is necessary not to be misled either by appearances or by temporary alliances. First of all, schools of political thought emerged only in a very few places. Individual thinkers may be found elsewhere from time to time, but it was only in England, France, Germany, and America that political thinking was practiced and published regularly. Then, among the large European countries, neither Russia nor Spain engaged significantly in political thinking, so that political events in these lands necessarily reflected imported ideas. Finally, one must place the British-French alliance in two world wars, as well as the temporary participation on our side by the Soviet Union, in the appropriate context.

The context is one of irreconcilable differences between two views of the world. One view, the Anglo-American, holds that human ability to comprehend, adjudicate, and arrange the world around us is limited; that the only attainable goal is continuously to improve the conditions which enable individuals to achieve their personal best. The other view, predominantly Franco-Germanic, places human reason at the center of our existence, claiming that certain people are capable of comprehending, adjudicating, and arranging the world around us; and that such people are called upon to guide all others toward an increasingly perfect and just world in which all desires will have been either eliminated or satisfied.

Traditional labels are the last obstacles in the path of understanding. Societies modeled on the Anglo-American line are often referred to as capitalist, or democratic, or classical-liberal. True to its tradition of using arbitrary and contradictory words to camouflage substance, the Franco-Germanic line has been known as statism, collectivism, socialism, fascism, nazism, communism, bolshevism, Maoism, or modern liberalism. The "-ism" in each label is significant. The need to paint the Anglo-American side also as an "-ism" led to the term "capitalism," which was proposed by those who oppose it.

It is inaccurate to use the label "capitalism" because all *other* "-isms" prescribe a set of conditions to which society must conform, if necessary through coercion or by force. Freedom of enterprise and guaranteed ownership, on the other hand, are prerequisites of general prosperity—something that needs to be there to begin with, and which leads to what Friedrich Hayek aptly describes as the "extended order of cooperation." Hayek further proposes that this extended order exceeds the ability of any person or group to organize, and that it can only evolve naturally under certain conditions. Such notions, of course, are anathema to proponents of the Franco-Germanic line who hold that effective planning is not only possible but also essential, and that it must be undertaken by those whom the noted thinker Thomas Sowell calls "The Anointed" in his book *The Vision of the Anointed.*

That is why the attempt is made here to reduce the two lines of thought to bare essentials and to dispense with misleading labels. By focusing upon the underlying concepts, seemingly unconnected events of the past and the present emerge as a logical sequence.

What began as a mildly sarcastic criticism of John Locke by Immanuel Kant grew into an full-blown intellectual confrontation by the mid-to-late nineteenth century. One side was preparing the ground for a closed, regulated, directed-from-the-top society, asserting that such societies would, by definition, be just. The other "muddled along" by trial and error, trusting that instinct and enlightened self-interest would correct aberrations and lead to continuous improvement. In economic terms, the first is a zero-sum proposition, necessitating the most stringent prescriptions with regard to the distribution of national product. The other is a tale of constantly accumulating wealth, providing increased access to a growing number of participants. The legal comparison is more revealing still. As discussed earlier, one is a matrix of codified laws to which all have to conform, and in which guilt or innocence is established by professional jurists; the other is an evolving collection of common law and precedents, in which verdicts are delivered by citizen juries.

THE ONSET OF PERMANENT WAR

With Marx—as the most visible proponent—on one side, the debate could not remain civilized. While John Stuart Mill subjects socialism to a detached examination and draws his conclusions after having considered everyone's interest, Karl Marx's attacks reveal a pronounced *animus* and portray society's future solely in terms of inner conflict. A mere assessment here, a call to arms there.

And the time came when the arms were taken up. World War I had its origins in many well-documented scenarios. But there can be no doubt that Germany wished to engage England on the battlefield. The attack on France had territorial and emotional, but no philosophical, implications. Britain was the long-term "archenemy," so characterized by the commander of the German armies, Falkenhayn, in a memorandum to the German emperor at Christmas 1915. "Germany can expect no mercy from this enemy, so long as he still retains the slightest hope of achieving his object," he wrote. Germany lost the war, but German ideas, and the bloody example of the French Revolution of 1789, came together decisively in the Russian Revolution of 1917. Lenin realized that only a new orthodoxy could supplant the Russian Orthodox Church in people's hearts, and he found it in German books.

Around 1920, the Franco-Germanic line split. For the very first time, the Ideology—now labeled Marxism or socialism or communism—was acquiring a position of real power in Russia. But what if someone did not like Marx? Or Russians? Or Jews, who began to play a prominent role in some socialist and communist movements? Or what if orthodox socialists did not like one of their own members?

Adolf Hitler found the answer in the National Socialist German Workers' Party which offered "Socialism for Antisemites." And Benito Mussolini, expelled from the official Italian Socialist Party, demonstrated that one man can form his own socialist party and simply call it another name. He chose "fascist" to imply some atavistic connection to ancient Rome. The civil war in Spain offered an opportunity for the two factions to support opposite sides and clash for the first time. It was a trial run for Stalin and Hitler—the two men who had come to personify the horrendous potential of Franco-Germanic political thought. In possession of an ideology that aimed at ruling the world, and that justified the application of any and all means in the pursuit of that goal, they knew that an open confrontation would be certain to occur sooner or later. But both hoped that it would be later. Both knew that their ultimate confrontation would still have to be with the English-speaking world, and they wanted to be in a position of maximum strength when that hour struck.

Meanwhile in Spain, the real loser was America. For the first time, Americans were conned into a confrontation that was taking place between their two enemies. For the first time, Americans were persuaded to take sides between two factions of an ideology equally hostile to their own way of thinking. And it was in Spain that, for the first time, Americans were seduced into thinking that communists were "good."

Hitler and Stalin called it a draw, signed a pact, and celebrated the old-fashioned way: by splitting Poland between them as had been the custom of Prussian kings and Russian czars. Because England had shown little resistance to his exploratory conquests, Hitler thought the time had come to decide the debate once and for all. But he neither reckoned with British resolve nor with the rite of passage that had taken place in the meantime, making America the undisputed defender of the faith. As Britain had done for centuries, the United States now guarded freedom on the high seas... and in people's hearts.

THE WAR GOES "COLD"

Germany lost once again, but not before Hitler, unwittingly, handed the Ideology two wild cards. By waging war both on the Jews of Europe and on the Soviet Union, he made it possible for countless writers, musicians, and artists to become communists by convincing themselves that they were simply anti-nazi. And the fanatic determination with which Soviet troops pursued Germany's armies all the way to Berlin persuaded Jews that Russia under communism was their friend and ally after all. Forgotten were the Russian pogroms, forgotten was Stalin's own rabid antisemitism, forgotten was the Hitler-Stalin pact. Troubled, moreover, by the thought of living in safety and comfort while their European relatives perished, Jews in America became easy targets for expertly-focused Soviet propaganda. When Stalin showed his real colors again by placing Berlin under blockade in 1948, he figured on little resistence by European opinion makers, and sufficient support from Americans who, one way or other, had caught the "red" virus between 1936 and 1948. He figured, also, on Anglo-American restraint, and rightly so: no nuclear ultimatum was issued to Russia. Instead, Berlin was supplied from the air until Stalin decided to call it a day.

But, like his one-time friend Hitler before him, Stalin did not comprehend the strength of basic Anglo-American resolve. In his famous Iron Curtain speech, on March 5, 1946, Winston Churchill had already warned all who would listen about the Soviet threat to the world. And a year later, President Harry Truman enunciated what became known as the Truman Doctrine, committing the United States to protecting Greece and Turkey against Soviet aggression. The combination of Anglo-American restraint and resolve saved the Western sectors of Berlin without a shot being fired.

Unmistakably, however, the next war—the Cold War—had begun.

The combination of apparent Anglo-American invincibility on the field of battle with Anglo-American political and economic thought appeared to hold the advantage. A special factor was the spread of the English language, which replaced even French, for centuries the international language of diplomats. German leadership in philosophy, literature, and technology notwithstanding, English became the language also of broadcast communications and aviation. Above all, seminal English phrases such as "my home is my castle," or "innocent until proven guilty" were insurmountable obstacles in the paths of all who sought to suppress the spirit of freedom.

Significantly, the spirit of freedom, this all-powerful language, and the growing network of English-speaking nations were now under the protection of Americans—people to whom failure was not even a possibility. There could be no hope of ever defeating "those Americans" on the battlefield.

Those Americans had to be *converted*.

THE LOSS OF AMERICA'S IMMUNITY

As the 1960s began, such hopes seemed more distant than ever. A young and dynamic John F. Kennedy introduced tax reductions, and the effect of these propelled the affluence of Americans to stratospheric levels. The failed Russian attempt to station nuclear missiles on Cuba increased America's national sense of well-being. A massive space program got under way, and included a commitment to send a manned mission to the moon. And the long-standing debt to the still-segregated black Americans in southern states was about to be retired. Opportunity, a majority agreed, had to be available on a truly equal basis.

It might have been another American success story. It was not to be.

The assassination of Kennedy, and its aftermath, threw the entire nation off balance. It seemed to paralyze thought and deed. A period of national daze set in. The substitute president, Lyndon B. Johnson, was more cunning, but had none of the stature of John F. Kennedy. And now, the traumatic turn of events stripped him of the know-how he was reputed to possess in significant quantities. He became obsessed with creating a place in history for himself that could compete with the shadow of his martyred predecessor. To this end, he abandoned every time-tested economic principle to build his "Great Society." To this end, he abandoned every time-honored military principle and waged war in Vietnam with no strategy to win it. To this end, he attempted to "manage" the civil rights movement, as he was used to managing the U.S. Senate. Together, these determinants erupted in a divergence of public opinion not seen since the Civil War.

Suddenly, unexpectedly, the stage seemed set for the conversion of America to some form of socialism. The opportunity was unmistakable. It brought together diverse forces—and they were formidable.

The other side could not believe its luck. A few years back, in 1956, communist parties in Europe had suffered their greatest setback. In rapid succession, Khrushchev had revealed details of

Stalin's bone-chilling personal terror. Then, fourteen-year-olds armed only with bottles of gasoline took on Soviet tanks on the streets of Budapest, exposing the desperation brought on by Soviet-Russian terror. Finally, the same Khrushchev who had appeared shocked by Stalin's methods, ordered Soviet tanks to roll over the children. French and Italian communists fled the Party in droves.

COMMUNISM'S NEW LEASE ON LIFE

But they were back now—and fortified, immeasurably, by German academia. After World War II, German academics, the backbone of the Third Reich, had lain low. Now the only direction left to them was the communist version of the Franco-Germanic line. They congregated around Martin Heidegger, the first nazi chancellor of a university who, in his 1933 maiden speech, demanded "the end of academic freedom." Still pursuing the objective of defeating the English-speaking world, Heidegger and German academia switched from the Nazi Party to orthodox Marxism, a not-so-difficult feat. At the end of World War II in Hungary, for example, the GPU (as the KGB was then called) took over the building the Gestapo had equipped for tortures and murders, and the personnel as well.

The Vietnam conflict, clearly America's own war with no UN umbrella, offered the perfect rallying point. In Berlin and in Korea, America had shown that it was willing to sacrifice—not to win, just to restore the *status quo*. Now Vietnam, too, looked like a stalemate. From stalemate it is only one step—though a big one—to defeat. Lenin taught that a lost war was the best prelude to revolution, for it would "[turn] the imperialist war into civil war."

Marxists of the world, old and new, were united in their resolve: America had to lose the war.

The stakes were even higher than that: Americans had to be taught that it was possible for them to lose a war.

Suddenly, such a possibility loomed because the American

generation that first dug itself out of the Great Depression, then dug the world out of the abyss of World War II, was followed by a very different generation. These young people had gotten everything without a struggle. Suffering from *ennui* brought on by affluence—"rebels without a cause" to borrow from the title of the James Dean film—they were easy prey for rebels *with* a cause. And rebellion was in full swing all over Western Europe, where proclaiming hatred for America became the leading spectator sport. High-profile anarchist Daniel Cohn-Bendit did not stop there. He issued a call "to rid ourselves of the Judeo-Christian ethic." Americans studying in England were the first to join weekly with the "rent-a-crowd" (as they became known) in anti-war protest rallies. In a parallel development, blueprints for the destruction of western civilization were unveiled by theorists such as Derrida, Marcuse, and members of the Frankfurt School.

The French Jacques Derrida, who not long ago assured a Riverside, California, audience that "there is no future without Marx," has been a leading transmitter of Martin Heidegger. Herbert Marcuse, after fleeing from Germany in 1934, found his new home in America. In the 1960s, as a member of the faculty at the University of California, he openly advocated the overthrow of American society by a minority and extolled the virtues of "the violence of revolutionary terror," directly and through disciples like Angela Davis. The so-called Frankfurt School unleashed a whole new torrent of words, openly contemptuous of the English-speaking world and pronouncing that "market economy is dead; planned economy has won." References to "American fascists" abounded.

Aided by New York's Institute for Social Research, America's enemies zeroed in on America's Achilles' heel: its conscience. Tell Americans they have done something "wrong," and you will command their attention. A whole army began to tell Americans that everything they did, everything they had done was, is, "wrong." Who were these people? In Europe, some simply resented U.S.

power, others viewed the United States as the impediment to "progress"; some, even, found America's largesse in victory an unbearable burden. In America, remnants of the communist-led Abraham Lincoln Battalion that fought in the Spanish Civil War now linked up with the civil rights movement and Hollywood. The motion picture industry never forgot the hearings by the House Committee on Un-American Activities (HUAC), and was primed to avenge it. If Americans still doubted that revolution or civil war was at hand, they were soon convinced by the evidence of exploding campuses and burning cities.

THE "ALMOST" REVOLUTION

A nation whose resolve proved more than a match in the face of German technological genius and Soviet numerical advantage seemed to have lost its footing at last. Stunned into a state of suspended animation by the upheavals and never-ending demands, Americans watched helplessly as the dollar plummeted from its fixed position, as the Arabs slapped on the first oil embargo, and as terrorists hijacked U.S. airliners with impunity. Every time a demand was met, two fresh ones grew in its place. Every time calmer heads seemed to prevail, a new fuse was lit.

Who prompted the demands? Who organized the upheavals? Who lit fuse after fuse? Was it all a conspiracy?

No. It was not a conspiracy in the sense of a small band of people meeting in a dark cellar, writing out a blueprint. It was not a process of subversion, although the Soviet Union expended vast sums on subversion. It was not even international communism acting in concert. It was *all* of these—and much more. It was a first opportunity to strike at the heart of the English-speaking world. Everybody with an ax to grind got into the act, and America's youth was whipped into a near-continuous state of hysteria by a judicious blend of drugs, sex, and propaganda.

And yet, to mention moments of greatest revolutionary potential, Chicago came and went. Kent State came and went. Even Watergate failed to dismantle the American government. The "Revolution" had failed.

But the instigators did not go empty-handed. They had succeeded in infecting Americans with three of Europe's chronic conditions, and these were decisive gains—gains that no effort, not even the passage of time, could reverse.

First among these was Fear. Because they had never lost a war, Americans were fearless. (Or is it because they were fearless that they never lost a war?) That was the transcendental significance of forcing the Vietnam defeat upon America. And, once lost, it is easy to reinforce the sense of fear. Repetition of the phrase, "I'm scared!" on screens big and small will do it.

The other source of previously impenetrable strength was the bond between Americans and their country—part pride, part warmth, part spirit. During the late 1960s that bond was destroyed for good in the minds of a generation, or a large proportion of it. For the first time, millions of Americans came to resent, to view with suspicion, in some cases actually to hate, America.

The third affliction had to do with uniforms. On the continent of Europe, a uniform had always produced a sense of power, a separation from the rest of one's countrymen. By contrast, Americans in uniform had been just like any other American, except in different clothes. Over two centuries, they had performed duties, all of which had been in the service of the people. They had not demanded respect—they earned it. Now, policemen were reviled as "pigs," and members of the armed forces were spat upon. Resentment and suspicion replaced what had been a sense of togetherness.

All this notwithstanding, the revolution failed in the immediate term. What was to be done? Once again, Lenin helped out. He had called it the "Salami Tactic." The recipe calls for a slice-by-slice approach, should the general onslaught stall. Indeed, the past twenty-five years have seen an incremental, systematic dismantling and replacement of the basic ingredients that made America, America. From a distance, much of the structure looks the same. But the foundations reveal extensive damage. That which earthquakes failed to inflict, termites now accomplish inch by inch, day by day.

Individual rights make up the foundations of liberty. Individual rights impose limitations on power. Individual rights had to be, indeed came to be, the first "slice of the salami." The dismantling of individual rights occurred through the establishment of group rights. And since group rights have no basis in law, their introduction ushered in the deconstruction of the Rule of Law.

Group rights, of course, necessitated the existence of groups. The only large group readily available in the 1960s was America's black population. In those days when impatience erupted from coast to coast, propagandists had a field day. No, it was not difficult to suggest that black Americans go their separate way, and remain a group.

But it was cruel; and it was criminal.

CHAPTER THIRTEEN

THINKING ABOUT BLACK AMERICANS

A TOUCH OF HONESTY

In today's America, no position in society carries a burden comparable to that of hard-working, successful, positive-thinking blacks. Official, though usually self-appointed, spokesmen for what they call "the black community" denounce the well-adjusted in harsh language. Non-black America pays lip service to their accomplishments, but few can completely disassociate achievers from the lingering negative image black people still invoke, even though most would be reluctant to admit to it. The many black Americans who, the burden notwithstanding, continue to strive, smile, and succeed, are owed far greater appreciation than they receive.

At the same time, the image has come to have less and less to do with racism. What is touted as racism is, in reality, a matter of those "balance sheets" we discussed earlier. While we all pay attention to individual balance sheets and formulate our *personal* relationships based on them, most of us simply cannot ignore the collective balance sheet of a group.

Whether or not we approve of it, the inclination to see people in groups is basic to human nature. Though we always allow for exceptions, we note and register group characteristics. Most of them, by inclination or habit, exist. And precisely because they exist, *we depend on individual rights* to make sure group characteristics do not have the last word in determining a person's fate. Without individual rights, individual accomplishment is severely hampered. Without individual accomplishment, the collective balance sheet dominates.

THE "EXPLANATIONS" GAME

Society has been spending vast amounts of financial and intellectual capital on trying to comprehend why people do or don't do things—why some can and others apparently cannot do certain things. The dispute proceeds under a variety of labels, such as "nature or nurture," "genetic or cultural," and "innate or acquired." In most cases, the answer should be, "Some of both, but we don't know for sure and, chances are, we never will."

No aspect of the foregoing debate is more frustrating than the perennial attempts to "explain" why much of America's black population is behind in many areas of activity. Every time a book takes up the topic, the media erupt with hysterical accusations of racism. These recurring clashes have their origins in two very different scenarios.

The first, we can trace back to the line that stretches from the Enlightenment through Marx, Darwin, Freud, and others who assume the existence of a logical scientific explanation for everything, as well as our ability to discern it. A more recent development is the growing tendency of closing our eyes to reality, and a corresponding escape into a make-believe world.

The debate has been framed in several different ways by such scholars as Charles Murray (*The Bell Curve*) or Dinesh D'Souza (*The End of Racism*)—two recent books that deal with race-related issues—but not in terms that acknowledge the limitations of human understanding, as well as the need to be both realistic and honest.

By way of explaining the problems of blacks, America has

considered genetic inferiority, exploitation of Africa by Europe, a "unique pathology," slavery, the diminished role of the church, continuing oppression of blacks, the welfare state, the "memory" of slavery, absentee fathers—just to mention a few. And the wild card, of course: white "racism."

Whatever the preferred explanation, whether the continuing impact of slavery or inferior genes, the troubling aspect of all these explanations is the underlying assumption that there is *something wrong* with black people. As long as we ask what is wrong with blacks, or *why* there is something wrong with blacks, we will continue to go around in circles. The assumption itself creates obstacles to a resolution. It is also an insult.

COMPARATIVE HISTORY

A common shortcoming is to define the unknown in terms of the known. For example, children are often told that the mammoth was an "early, irregular version" of the elephant. In a similar fashion, whites regard the evolution and development of European (western) civilization as the norm, and have a compulsive need to apply it as the yardstick for scenarios that are utterly different.

Here, then, is a different and unorthodox view of the "black" scenario. For the most part, people in Africa, especially in sub-Saharan Africa, have lived at peace with their surroundings. They neither questioned the provisions of Nature nor expended significant efforts to alter them. There was no perceptible attempt to improve circumstances, and no urge to explore beyond their immediate surroundings. People of non-African ancestry treat this as a negative entry on the African balance sheet, as if Africans had "failed," or fallen short of expectations. In response, some black leaders have made exhaustive attempts to invent people, circumstances, and accomplishments that have nothing to do with reality. If, instead, both sides could simply accept and live with the facts and cease trying to evaluate, explain, excuse, or renounce the past, we would be taking a significant step in the right direction.

Another useful step would be a realistic comparison of the people who populated the thirteen colonies at the time of America's founding. In the course of the seventeenth and eighteenth centuries, a large number of African people were brought to the place that was to become the United States, a place where they did not choose to be. They were in bondage and forced to toil in a strange land. And they were surrounded by people who were not only adventurous and motivated, but exceptionally so.

None of us is equipped to judge whether it is a good thing to live in constant quest for something different—even if you believe that the "different" will be "better"—or to leave well enough alone. Who is to say which condition makes for greater contentment? (Most of mankind lives oblivious to what we call "the great contributions to mankind.") Still, regardless of value systems, an honest look reveals a huge discrepancy between the colonists and the slaves. The former stood on the shoulders of generations stretching back to the beginnings of written history, themselves carrying on the tradition of exploring, altering, and growing. The latter stemmed from places where the kinds of developments that brought European colonists to North America had not even begun. The paths of existence diverged over thousands of years. Imagine two lines that begin to diverge ever so slightly. Now imagine the distance between them after thousands of years.

MORE HONESTY

It may offend disciples of the Franco-Germanic school of thought (these days in America they call themselves "liberals"), but bridging thousands of years is a slow and painstaking process. There is a story about the Texas millionaire who becomes so enamored of the velvet emerald of English lawns that he asks his host, lord of the manor, to disclose the secret. His lordship has the head gardener come and write out a list of the correct seeds, fertilizers, frequency of watering, and method of mowing. Next year, the Texan visits again. "How is your lawn?" his host inquires. "Best in the whole great state of Texas, let me tell you," comes the answer, "but not even close to yours." The gardener is called again. "Did you follow *all* my instructions, sir?" he asks. "To the letter!" the guest replies. "Very well, sir. You need to continue doing just that for about five hundred years. Then you'll have a lawn like this."

From the time people first thought of writing, it took over five thousand years to arrive, as America did, at a stage of high general literacy. From the invention of the wheel, it took more than five thousand years to think of the automobile.

Most of the so-called "problems with the black community" stem from the initial divergence, and the time it is taking for the lines to converge—to "get in synch." Remarkably, however, a large number of black Americans have fast become indistinguishable from the rest of America, except for their skin color. And their accomplishments have received but a fraction of the appreciation and respect owed them.

Indeed, millions have succeeded. And there could be millions more. That there are not, and the importance of understanding why there are not, is half the reason for this chapter. The other half is the realization that individual rights—the key to our liberty—may become a distant memory if we do not find ways to alter the destructive course we presently pursue.

OBSTACLES TO INTEGRATION

Like most of our troubles, it all began in the 1960s. At the moment when equal opportunity at last opened up for blacks, contrary efforts got under way to drive the black population off the American track. All manner of separatist avenues, such as the Nation of Islam, were proposed by black leaders to forestall integration. In *The Shadow of the*

Panther: Huey Newton and the Price of Black Power in America, Hugh Pearson reminds us of encountering (as a third grader in Fort Wayne, Indiana) the leather jackets—a straight carry-over of the uniform worn by both nazi and bolshevik paramilitary units—the balled-fist communist salute, and the preoccupation with the "lumpen proletariat," a special category within the Marxist-Leninist doctrine.

Most harmful of all, however, was the adoption of the "African" label and its accessories. If the objective is integration, why create an artificial nationality? If the objective is not integration, what was the civil rights movement all about?

Being "African" in America amounts to an artificial nationality. There really is no such thing as an "African-American." People so designated are "Americans-whose-distant-ancestry-is-somewhere-on-the-African-continent." Realistically, people whose families have been in America for five, six, seven, or more generations do not have roots elsewhere. "So what, if tales of great African kings, princes, and wealth make people happy?" is the next question.

That very question could be posed about drugs. The invention of a past that never was is a kind of drug. It lulls the recipient into a false sense of satisfaction and removes the urgency of paying attention to the present. While the obsession with Africa's past is a matter of choice, being held accountable for what people do, or do not do, here and now is unavoidable. For this reason, attention ought to be focused on current balance sheets. Instead, time and energy is wasted by filling in some blank spaces with fictitious data. Does such an approach promise a high probability of success? The practice, once again, was inherited from the Third Reich ("everything has been written or invented by Germans") and the Soviet Union ("everything has been discovered or invented by Russians"). Then, because enough people knew better, the ultimate result was simply ridicule.

The same is not true of Afro-centric teaching. Those who are at the receiving end are often young and often do not know better. This is their first and only source of information. Teaching fiction to them is an unforgivable abuse of education. Worst of all is the complicity of many in white America who tacitly acquiesce to it or even support it. What possible long-term benefit could this fiction bring? If it is about the much-touted "self-esteem," surely America, of all places, cares little about past status, but all the more about present accomplishment. Indeed, millions came here hoping to shed the burdens of their collective balance sheets—partly to build an individual one, partly to share in America's own. If a Hungarian immigrant who arrived here at the age of twenty-two can look upon Washington, Jefferson, Franklin, and Madison as the founders of *his* country, why not a person whose ancestors were actually here when the country was founded?

Because, comes the obligatory answer, slaves were not included in America's founding.

Yes, they were.

How else could the descendants of slaves come to share in the liberties, the opportunities, the riches of America?

SLAVERY AND AFRO-CENTRICITY

Slavery did not happen overnight, and it was not invented in America. For millennia, it had been the standard way of organizing society. Comparatively speaking, slavery in North America was a minor blip in history. Ancient Egypt was another matter. Those who extol Egypt's contributions to mankind need to remember the enslaved millions who died like flies while hauling stone for the pyramids. And, as Voltaire recalls in the *Philosophical Letters*, the English themselves had been slaves to a succession of slave keepers.

Why do many of the same people who talk incessantly about slavery in America's past find nothing reprehensible about present-day slavery in the Sudan, Nigeria, or Gabon?

But nothing is as troubling as the NAACP's current plan to turn away from integration. Americans have been living with busing, affirmative action, and even quotas for the sake of integration. Was it all for nothing?

Integration as a concept has not failed. The demagoguery of the self-appointed prophets of all skin colors is what has failed. Integration remains the only way so long as it is pursued and nurtured with the use of reason. Does anyone believe that whipping up the sentiments of black Americans against the country in which they are supposed to succeed will *help* them succeed? And, if hope for success is not the reason for whipping up the sentiments, what is?

Even if Liberia had been an unqualified success, the idea of a return to Africa is a mirage. Americans belong in America, and no amount of role-playing will make a difference. Neither the celebration of Kwaanza nor make-believe African names will change reality. Reality is that the person now calling himself Kweisi Mfume would no more trade his life in America for one in Africa than the rest of us. Reality is that, despite growing up in Hungary, despite maintaining contact, despite ease with the language, I would find it nearly impossible to move back. Reality is that the few black Americans who do go to Africa usually return with memories they would sooner not have, as those described recently by Keith Richburg in his book, *Out of America: A Black Man Confronts Africa*.

Meanwhile the wholly fictitious propaganda and the industry that has sprung up around it is inflicting great harm. A kind of gulag is being forged in America, and a hostile one at that. When I first arrived in 1959, it was impossible not to be struck by the friendliness of black faces. During the past thirty years, the change to hostility has been as impossible to ignore.

AFFIRMATIVE ACTION—A TRAP

The constant barrage about "racism" on television, or in speeches by members of Congress and others in public life, ought to be cause for concern. Even if it were true, the "America the Horrible" approach would be counterproductive, unless those engaged in it wish to bring about a major confrontation. Do they?

Equally counterproductive are racial quotas in any form. As well as undermining the very foundations of America, such practices deprive blacks of the opportunity of real progress. The proper comprehension of cause and effect is at the heart of success. From earliest times, Americans learned the penalties for doing poorly, the rewards for doing well. Today, too many black Americans are shielded from that vital lesson. There is also too much attention focused on *being there*, at the expense of *getting from here to there*. In other words, poor black children see the affluence of the "white" world, but they are rarely told about the struggle, the suffering, the effort, the sacrifice, and the determination that preceded the achievement. What then will cause the collective balance sheet to improve?

Improving the collective balance sheet alone will bring about improvement in the long-term relationship of people. Where are the societies that have succeeded by placing incompetent people in high positions? The nazis, goodness knows, tried it by *restricting* the percentage of Jews. The bolsheviks tried it by *prescribing* the percentage of workers and peasants. Where are they now?

Affirmative action is not only counterproductive in the practical sense; it is also insupportable in the theoretical sense. America's founding principles still offer the best deal. No one has come forward with anything better than equality before the law.

REALITY, REALITY

No sudden discovery of ancient African inventions, no special African-American corners in museums, no amount of affirmative-action cabinet members can do a fraction of the good that a new participatory approach would elicit. To hear great aspirations articulated in place of growing demands would be nothing less than revolutionary.

It would also be most encouraging to hear praise by black speakers lavished on black Americans who are doing an outstanding job today, rather than listening to their condemnation for being "Uncle Toms" and "Oreos." As long as prominent black Americans continue to insist on a black America, and on defining it in terms of its least successful layer, they impel everyone else to adopt the same standards. It would be worth a try to portray black America in terms of its successes, which in many cases are extraordinary. Of course, such a turn would necessitate the recognition that succeeding in western civilization is possible only in terms of western civilization. But to believe otherwise is a sure sign of Compartmentalized Brain Syndrome.

Further, such a turn would necessitate the study of *real* history. Much unhappiness among black Americans emanates from mistaken perceptions as to when and how white Americans became affluent. The fact is, most people have had a difficult life on this planet. The settlers of America were not offered air-conditioned homes with full refrigerators and gassed-up automobiles. The pilgrims, the pioneers, and the homesteaders paid their dues. So did the builders of industry, the Depression generation, and the waves upon waves of immigrants. Today there are millions in Europe who would gladly swap economic conditions with the "dispossessed" of America's inner city. As opposed to most other places, opportunity in America is, has been, and remains just around the corner. As opposed to most places, effort in America is almost certain to be rewarded. And that is the blessing we must not relinquish under any circumstances.

And that is why the nation is indebted to the millions of black Americans who have committed themselves and their families to a course that, for the time being, is a thankless one. Black Americans represent the ultimate confirmation of America's ability to unlock humanity's potential to the fullest extent. They demonstrate daily that there is life outside the "group." They predicate their success on individual effort and accomplishment, proving that individual rights and equal standing before the law are all one really needs. As America's future course hangs in the balance, the significance of their effort cannot be overrated. Group rights—the erosion of individual rights—began with black group rights. If we hope to reverse the malignancy of privilege, a majority of black Americans will first have to realize that individual rights offer their only long-term guarantee for the pursuit of happiness.

PROPERTY

CHAPTER FOURTEEN

BRASS TACKS

TWO "ZONES"

All those who cause the erosion of individual rights by demanding, advocating, or promoting group rights are engaged, consciously or not, in dismantling the United States of America as we know it. So are all those who interfere with the right of people to acquire, hold, or dispose of property, and to enter into contract freely with one another. There may be differences of degree, but persons so inclined are traveling in the same direction—be they card-carrying communists, members of the United States Congress (from either party), or the president himself. The journey takes place between the two ends of the political road: America's founding principles at one, communism at the other.

Nothing has been as consistently harmful as the fallacy that "fascism" (itself a misnomer) and communism represent opposite extremes. However traditional, however well established, the use of "right" and "left" as political designations serves only to confuse. As discussed in some detail, fascism/nazism and bolshevism/socialism are all branches of the same tree. They cannot possibly represent "right" and "left" respectively since, under proper scrutiny, they all reveal the same basic characteristics. In this, we refer to no less an authority than Vladimir Ilyich Lenin, who wrote an entire book on the topic and called it *Leftism: Communism's Infantile Disorder*. Indeed, the choices Americans must make would be a great deal easier if "truth in labeling" were applied to the political process. But since confusing terminology has always been effective as a weapon, any attempt to recast the political vocabulary would meet with massive resistance. The effort, nonetheless, ought to be made because the current terminology clearly favors those who are traveling *away* from America's founding principles.

Again and again, it must be pointed out that "communism" is the designation used here for the opposite end of the road leading away from America's founding principles, because none other is available. *Communism has been defined as a state to be achieved*, whereas the terms "American liberalism," "searching for social justice," or "leftist" describe attitudes—means by which to get there. Public ownership of the tools of production, a much-cited ingredient of socialism, also falls into the category of means, not of ends. To continue the metaphor of portraying America's founding principles and communism as two "zones" connected by a lengthy road, a majority of Americans prefer to be seen somewhere along that road. Few would admit to being outright communists in the privacy of their home, much less in public. Those who profess to reside in the American "zone" are more numerous and more vocal. They call themselves "conservative," and are the subject of daily ridicule in the media and elsewhere.

DELUSIONS

But the largest segment of Americans has come to engage in self-delusion of one sort or another. One of the popular and accepted ways is by using the term "economic conservative—social liberal," and its variants, such as "economic conservative—social moderate," or "economic conservative with a social conscience." We saw early on how the word "social," as a qualifier, made nonsense of a phrase—so with the above. "Social" does not mean tolerance or compassion. When the word was imported from Germany (and France), it merely confused and polluted our vocabulary. Today, the "social" half of a phrase stands for approval of certain government controls over society and reveals the hypocrisy of the statement. If government intrusion is accepted, it will not be confined to any one area. Government needs money to operate its "social" policies, and it can obtain money only if it exercises powers not specified in the Declaration of Independence, and not granted in the Constitution. How the exercise of such powers becomes acceptable to an "economic conservative" is where the self-delusion occurs.

History does not stand still. As Heraclitos of ancient Greece remarked, "One cannot step twice into the same river." Whether as individuals or as a society, we are in constant motion. And motion has direction. Individually or collectively, every political step we take moves us either closer to, or farther away from, America's founding principles. Every time we move away from the "American" zone, we are moving toward the other zone we call "communism" by default. Is everyone who moves toward communism a communist? That depends. If by "communist" we still mean people who go around unkempt and unshaven, or who carry the *Daily Worker*, the answer is no. If by "communist" we mean people who would haul off "class enemies" to detention camps and countenance executions without trial, the answer is still no. But if by communist we mean people who tell us what we may and may not say, who cause children to inform on their parents, and who assume the power to confiscate our property—the answer might well be different.

PROPERTIES OF PROPERTY

Property—in all its forms, including one's earnings—holds the key. At one time or another, many might stray from the American "zone," pulled away by reading a book, hearing a lecture, witnessing poverty, and so on. The absolute guarantee of property is the powerful magnet that will keep everyone within proximity of the American zone and ensure that *society* remains securely anchored in it, the straying of individuals notwithstanding. So long as people are unwilling to give up their property, so long as governments will not take property without compensation, society will never be cast adrift. It will remain immune to the pull exerted by the opposite end.

Most of us know Jefferson's famous quote ("Property is the foundation of all civilized society") or Madison's ("The protection of these faculties [different and unequal faculties of acquiring property] is the first object of Government"). There is another by Lord Camden, from a 1766 speech in the British House of Lords: "The [omnipotence of the legislature] cannot take away any man's private property without making him compensation." But it was a childhood friend who, inadvertently, illuminated the supreme importance of property. Like myself, this friend left Hungary many years ago to escape communism. Unlike myself, he did so in good time, before the Iron Curtain came down. Eventually he ended up in Washington, D.C., running the international department of a major law firm. He went on to earn huge sums of money by negotiating worldwide business deals. But with regard to domestic politics, he spoke like a liberal. Somewhere in his heart my friend must have known better because he became an avid reader (and commentator) of everything I wrote. Unexpectedly, we seemed to agree in most instances, until he read a speech of mine about the founding principles. The speech included the unconditional guarantee of property. My friend could not get over this one point. Ill as he was by then, he nonetheless wrote message after message, admonishing me for saying that property was an absolute. He contended that it cannot be absolute, that it *must* not be—even though his entire professional and personal existence was predicated on the guarantee of property.

As the communist end depends on the denial of property, so the

American end requires the absolute guarantee of it. Once the right to acquire, hold, or dispose of property becomes conditional, so does everything else that constitutes the core of America. Man's struggle across the ages could be portrayed as the struggle by the weak against the ability of the strong to take away their property. The Tenth Commandment sought to rein in this impulse when it admonished the Israelites not to covet their neighbor's house or wife, or anything else of their neighbor's. Ever practical, the English made provisions for corresponding secular laws, just in case man's willingness to obey the commandments should take an eternity to emerge. The Magna Carta's main thrust addressed property laws. From 1215 onward, English liberties flourished, while on the Continent of Europe the struggle had not even begun.

Experience shows property and liberty to be inseparable. Indeed, one might conclude that liberty is a function of property guaranteed. This is so because, in the broadest sense, everything may be seen as a person's property—even life itself. *Invariably, those societies that indulged in the large-scale, "legal" taking of lives, started by taking property through government action.*

METHODS AND ORIGINS

Because property cannot be "almost guaranteed," the bond that ties people and their possessions must be whole. Once a gap is made and is tolerated, the effect is not unlike a fruit penetrated by the first worm.

In any attempt to separate people from their possessions, "free" societies must employ methods different from "unfree" societies. Since "free" societies, by definition, guarantee property, first a breach must be made, and then carefully, slowly it must be widened. Once the "worm" has penetrated, universally tested methods of expropriating property become applicable. To understand the process fully, it is beneficial to study the two regimes where those methods were taken to their ultimate degree, and see whether recent developments in

America show any similarity. The two regimes, of course, are Germany's Third Reich and Russia's Soviet Union. The first benefit is to realize that the two, indeed, were twins. The second, and greater, benefit derives from grasping the similarities, if any, between them and present trends in America. Such similarities would further prove the existence of only two schools of political thought.

Those who are actually committed to guiding America away from its origins, and closer and closer to communism, are likely to be studying the same two regimes. On a conscious level, they would vehemently deny any connection to national-socialist (nazi) practices. On a conscious level, they would concede that the Soviet Union made many "mistakes." But the question remains: where do currently dominant legislative, executive, and judicial attitudes originate? If not in America's founding principles, then the obvious—the only—alternative sources are the doctrines that produced the national-socialist/communist regimes. Acceptance of reality will be easier if we remember that truly new ideas are rare indeed. And if our "age of abundance" reveals exceptional poverty in any one realm, it is in the realm of fresh ideas.

When the president of the United States—or any other political leader of current vintage—launches a "new initiative," it may be assumed to have come from an old book. That explains partly why American officials support the current frenzied revisionism of history: new generations should never suspect the true origins of those initiatives. All the more reason for the rest of us to be constantly aware of the system that awaits at the other end of the road. All the more reason for the rest of us to know emotionally as well as rationally that every position we take is a move in one direction or the other.

CHAPTER FIFTEEN

FRATERNAL TWINS

MIRROR IMAGES

Midnight. Fists were banging on the door.

"Open up," yelled the crude voice. As the father of the family unlocked the door with trembling hands, he took in the sight of three men in shiny leather jackets.

"You and your lot have thirty minutes to pack necessities. Get on with it!"

The children were crying, the mother tried to comfort them. There was no time to waste. Important papers, toothbrushes, cans of food, a bar of soap, and some warm clothing were crammed into bags small enough to carry. Everything else had to be left behind.

"Get going; we haven't got all year," shouted one of the men.

"Where are you taking us?"

"You'll know soon enough," snapped another.

They were members of the Arrow Cross Party, an offshoot of Germany's National Socialists. The year was 1944.

Midnight. Fists were banging on the door.

"Open up," yelled the crude voice. As the father of the family unlocked the door with trembling hands, he took in the sight of three men in shiny leather jackets.

"You and your lot have thirty minutes to pack necessities. Get on with it!"

The children were crying, the mother tried to comfort them. There was no time to waste. Important papers, toothbrushes, cans of food, a bar of soap, and some warm clothing were crammed into bags small enough to carry. Everything else had to be left behind.

"Get going; we haven't got all year," shouted one of the men.

"Where are you taking us?"

"You'll know soon enough," snapped another.

They were members of the Political Police, an offshoot of Russia's GPU (a.k.a. the NKVD). The year was 1949.

But that was in Hungary. And in Germany. And in Russia. Surely, such images have no bearing on life in the United States of America—a sovereign republic that lives by its Constitution. Then why bring it up?

Because the men in the shiny leather jackets were merely administering "social justice."

As part of our discussion about property, we have to comprehend how human beings come to be like the ones in the shiny leather jackets.

Beginning with the French Revolution of 1789, mass slaughter was instituted to fulfill the noble purpose of social justice. There is a measure of primordial honesty in the way people in Africa or Asia kill one another by the millions. By contrast, in Europe, they first write books about it. Grand reasons are offered by persons of self-proclaimed integrity, as in this passage from Adolf Hitler's *Mein Kampf*: "...as a freedom-loving man, I could not even conceive of any possibility of government other than parliament, for the idea of any sort of dictatorship would... have seemed to me a crime against freedom and all reason." Gradually, a different and "superior" path is discovered as, for example, a "truly Germanic" democracy, or a

"Soviet Socialist" republic, installed to replace the now derided "democratic parliamentarianism." Next, the need arises for "certain measures" that must be taken for "the people's own good." While some of these measures "may appear drastic," they are always said to be of a "temporary nature, until the conditions that demanded their application have been corrected." Sound familiar? Indeed. This same rationale is offered for many a current American practice, such as racial quotas.

As we look at the parallel practices of Nazi Germany and Soviet Russia, readers will recognize their similarities with trends in today's America.

FOUNDATIONS OF TYRANNY

The first order of business was to establish groups of "good" people and "evil" people. Part of this process was to instill the notion that those designated as "evil" were beyond redemption. Evil people had to be clearly identified and identifiable. The best authority, again, is Adolf Hitler. In *Mein Kampf* he tells us that "a great number of basically different enemies must always be described as belonging to the same group, so that as far as the mass of your followers is concerned, the battle is being waged against a single enemy. This strengthens the belief in the rightness of your cause...."

Hitler, as we know, decided upon "inferior races." Lenin chose "exploiter classes." Both began by apportioning blame to their selected targets—blame for everything that was disliked by the masses—and by indicating that there could be no improvement so long as the "evil people" retained influence. Invariably, this influence would be attributed to the possessions acquired at the expense of the "good" people. The stigma of "unfairly acquired" possessions was attached not merely to tangible things, but to property of every kind, including education and personal accomplishments. The hatred—whipped to a frenzy within an amazingly short period of time—spilled over onto the entire value system ("culture" is the currently fashionable term) of the targeted group. That way, all vestiges of the evil group could be eliminated. Remember, the thrust of Franco-Germanic political thought, the object of the search for social justice, is always "to eliminate."

First in importance was eliminating the right of evil people to their property. Carefully prepared by the barrage of blame hurled at the target group, ownership by them was no longer regarded as legitimate. That which civilized society would classify as acts of plunder acquired legitimacy because "evil people had come by their possessions through evil means." They—Jews in Germany, exploiters in Russia—were not entitled to the fruits of their "evil deeds." Detailed histories of individual "wrongdoing" assured daily replenishing of the wellspring of hatred. Little did the rest of society realize that wrenching property from the "evil people" was only the start, that they would be next. This Marxist approach to ownership was just as valid in the Third Reich as in the Soviet Union: The Program of the National Socialist German Workers' Party demanded "the nationalization of all business enterprises that have been organized into corporations."

The indispensable opposite of the evil person was the ideal person, who led the fight for the perfect world, and provided the model for the masses. Readers may be surprised to learn that the "Aryan Hero" of the Third Reich had its exact counterpart in the "Soviet Man." Both were to be worshiped.

The common agenda of the two regimes—underlying all doctrines, procedures, and operations—demanded that unlimited discretionary powers be concentrated in the hands of a small, self-perpetuating group in which membership was by invitation only. Members of the group typically fell into two categories: one of these purported to know what was best for all people; the other simply wanted unchecked power. The synergy was perfect: ideologues needed terrorists to retain physical control; terrorists needed ideologues to supply explanations for the rule they maintained. It was only natural that the objective was always to expand the number of those over whom power was exerted. And the ultimate objective, of course, was to concentrate all power in the hands of a single group. That is why competing formations assumed different labels for themselves—"National Socialist," "communist," "bolshevik," "fascist," "Maoist"—and a somewhat different outward appearance. They fully expected to fight it out until only one of them remained.

A SHARED BLUEPRINT

While the labels might have been different, the methods were identical. Successful exercise of power required not only control of the military and the police, but control of key institutions to replace, or supplement, brute force. The checklist included news sources—especially the visual variety—education, the judiciary, labor organizations, arts and entertainment, as well as a parental relationship between government and governed. Required, also, was the attribution of superhuman status to a Hitler, a Lenin, or a Mao. This had more to do with the need for infallibility at the top than with a particular person. The leader replaced the object of religious worship, just as secular celebrations of a political nature were positioned in the calendar to replace religious ones. The names of streets, towns, and institutions were also replaced. The double purpose: to do away with reminders of the past—thus discontinuing history—and to provide constant reminders of the present.

The practice of discontinuing history was indispensable. As noted before, successive generations had to be prevented from drawing possible parallels between past and present. This necessitated revision of the *entire* academic curriculum, lest another subject "accidentally" provide accurate information about history. And this, in turn, led to the reorientation of the entire educational system. While adults needed to be threatened in order to "forget" what they had learned, information could simply be withheld from young people and/or manipulated before it reached them. Sciences are exact, but the humanities are a propaganda minister or commissar's dream of a tool. Literature, the arts, sociology, and—above all—history provide unlimited opportunities for deleting certain facts, inserting trivial or fictitious names and events, attaching politically motivated interpretations, and changing any of these at will.

The framework was provided by creating youth organizations, identical in nature, in which membership was compulsory—except when exclusion was used as an instrument of humiliation. These organizations (Hitler Youth, Komsomol, Pioneers) provided access to the minds of people at a young age, ensured their early allegiance to the ideology and to the leader, and placed them under the command of a political appointee whose authority superseded that of the parental home, as well as of the school. Finally, teaching faculties were subordinated to operatives of the political organization whose "higher education" often consisted of six weeks at a Party school.

The corruption of education was matched by the corruption of the legal system. This required judges who would subordinate both their natural and acquired sense of justice to what was "the higher interest of the community" on a given day. Marching orders were best described by Hans Frank, president of the Academy of German Law and of the National Bar Association in the Third Reich:

> The basis for interpreting all legal sources is the National Socialist Philosophy, especially as expressed in the Party program.

Thus was born the activist judge who wore the robe as a uniform, similar to the black shirt, the brown shirt, or the red shirt. Some of them would hide behind recent laws which they were merely "implementing." Precisely for this reason, Americans today beware of laws enacted to elicit politically, rather than morally and ethically, desirable behavior.

Controlling the behavior of the adult population required the most sophisticated approach, if outright terror was to be relaxed to any extent. Although Lenin and Stalin pointed the way and Mao Tse-Tung achieved the ultimate by making one billion people wear the same clothes, it was the Germans—ever the theoreticians—who supplied the terminology for the first ingredient. They called it *Gleichschaltung*, or "switching to parity"—the twentieth-century German equivalent of France's "Egality" of 1789. *Gleichschaltung* called for total alignment with the goals of national-socialist policies and placed everyone on the same level, made everyone a cog in the giant wheel of the State.

Gleichschaltung operated on structural and cultural levels. Structurally, the first victim was federalism: within days of Hitler's accession, the states had to cede authority to the central government. Next, the leadership and membership of every kind of organization had to become politically and racially correct. The task of implementing structural changes was assigned to a variety of agencies and, as early as March 1933, a separate cabinet department was created for Josef Goebbels to oversee every aspect of the cultural scene, to make certain that *it* was politically correct. They used different terminology, but the reality of both the Soviet Union and the Third Reich was the great flattening which was in full progress from the very first day. Since it was not possible to raise anyone up by *fiat*, the alternative was to force everyone down.

It is astonishing and frightening how little time it took both in Russia and in Germany to accomplish this task. Demolishing what centuries have built does not require even a single generation.

TOOLS OF MANIPULATION

The next ingredient had to do with groups. While it may appear contradictory to identify groups in a society having just experienced *Gleichschaltung*, contradictions do not represent obstacles in a totalitarian structure. Assigning identity to groups was just as necessary as the leveling had been. Combined, the two approaches provided the means by which to maintain positive and negative imaging. The constant dichotomy of egalitarianism and group hatred proved to be a manipulative tool as simple as it was ingenious. Hitler used race and nationality, Lenin and Stalin mostly class—the outcome was the same.

Conscientious resistance was neutralized by choosing the loftiest slogans from the past as cover for government (party) policies, making anyone who opposed them the object of disdain or ridicule. Surely no one but a moron would reject the notions of "Liberty," "Equality," "Social Justice," or "Peace"—or argue against "National Unity" or "International Brotherhood." When necessary, people were publicly shamed into submission through having their positions twisted until they appeared to be opposing social justice. The practice of self-criticism was enforced so as to increase the subjects' "sensitivity" and awareness of their shortcomings, resulting in "improved attitudes." Once humiliated and cleansed, membership in "the master race" (if they were German), or being "a model for all humanity" (if Russian) awaited them.

On the subject of words, it is essential to comprehend the importance language occupies in the totalitarian state. Words, of course, reflect upon and determine attitudes in every society. But totalitarian states depend greatly on demagoguery which requires that formerly innocent words be given a tendentious political charge. The nazis and bolsheviks actually created their own respective glossaries of terms and prescribed with menacing precision which words were and which were not to be used, until people learned that the safest avenue was to remain silent. Thus, after all the vocabulary was under their control, it was unnecessary formally to outlaw freedom of speech.

FEAR

All of this required round-the-clock enforcement. For this reason, the Gestapo became a "state within the state," as was the Cheka/GPU/NKVD/KGB. Their responsibility was not merely to control, but to maintain a permanent state of fear. Still, internal security organs, however large, could not alone see to that. Therefore, in one sense or another everyone was recruited to be an agent of fear. In Nazi Germany, as in Soviet Russia, children were encouraged to inform on their parents, and neighbors on each other. Soon it became a matter of reporting someone before someone reported you. It was possible to be reported for virtually anything, so that people grew fearful of doing or saying common, ordinary things. One could never be sure whether somebody might "put a spin" on the most innocent act or remark.

Many a German and American film of the postwar period portrayed families in which a child becomes completely infatuated with the Hitler-Youth movement and its local leader, and keeps the entire family trembling. I recall, in particular, the actual case of a Hungarian family during the Soviet occupation. The father worked for the capital transportation cooperative, the mother in some factory. They had two children. One of them, a ten-year-old boy, was questioned at school about his home life. He related that his parents went to church on Sundays and made the children go, too. Next day, the father lost his job. All citizens were required to carry an identity book in which people's educational and employment histories were recorded. An entry showing dismissal of this sort meant that the person would never be employed elsewhere. That evening, the father killed his wife, his children, then himself. An extreme example, but not an isolated one in societies where children are recruited to inform on their parents.

"GET THEM YOUNG"

The dissolution of the family, already well under way as a result of the youth organizations and the reliance on children to monitor their (often less "progressive" or "reactionary") parents, was further accelerated by "producing" babies in untraditional ways. In Germany this was done by having pedigreed Aryans, usually SS soldiers, impregnate healthy women. In Soviet territories, glory was conferred upon girls giving birth outside wedlock. The delineation of duties was best summed up by Anton Semionovitch Makarenko, the leading Soviet expert on education, in his advice to parents about the way they ought to bring up their (own) children:

> It is not at all a matter of indifference to society what kind of people they will be. In handing over to you a certain measure of social authority, the Soviet state demands from you correct upbringing of future citizens.

And, to limit not only the authority but also the potential influence of parents on their children, daycare centers replaced the home environment. In them, supervisors trained by the state ensured correct behavior.

ENEMIES

A particularly important place in the political matrix was assigned to those considered to be enemies of the regime. Whereas democracies associate the word "enemy" with a physical attack on their territory or the threat thereof, national socialism and communism *require* the existence of enemies—internal and external—at all times. The selection of internal enemies (Jews in Germany, "exploiters" in Russia) would suggest a difference between the two regimes. But the Russians had anti-Jewish pogroms long before Hitler and, later, significant numbers of Jews were exiled or killed under the label "exploiter." Then too, for centuries, Prussia and Russia had laid claim to Poland; continuing the tradition, the Third Reich and the Soviet Union took turns inciting hatred toward Poles. Nazis—who were, after all, socialists—viewed aristocrats with the same hostility as the Soviets. And the Church, again, was looked upon by both as an enemy for the obvious reason that it, too, required allegiance and obedience—an attitude reserved exclusively to the party. "National Socialist and Christian concepts are irreconcilable," Martin Bormann stated as he began the Third Reich's authoritative statement on the subject.

While closer inspection points to similarities among internal enemies, examination of nazism and bolshevism's external enemies proved the most revealing. As discussed, the primary enemy in the eyes of both nazis and communists was, and is, the English-speaking world in all its manifestations. As countries switched from nazi occupation to Soviet occupation, it was not unusual for the same henchmen to jail the same persons for the same offense: listening to an English-language broadcast.

THE "UPSIDE-DOWN" SOCIETY

Having earlier reviewed the common roots, and, now, some of the common practices, let us turn to the impact of these practices upon people individually, and upon society as a whole. Most of us are aware of the deadly phrases, "Jews cannot step outside their race," and "Manufacturers, shopkeepers, and peasants with more than a few acres of land, cannot transcend their class." Such pronouncements justified the elimination of countless millions. But most of us are unaware of the fate both regimes meted out to those who continued to live and work where they always had—the "good" people, the "beneficiaries" of social justice.

First off, *Gleichschaltung* taught them to know their place. Alert to the continous presence of the internal security forces, they lived in constant fear of inadvertent words or actions. The people around them who wore a uniform (or just a shiny leather jacket), they soon learned, were their jailers, not their protectors. People in uniform, supplemented by those who sat at a desk in assorted government departments, served the "higher interest of the state." So did the courts—no hope for relief from there. As Hitler remarked, "We must exterminate the idea that it is the judge's function to let the law prevail(...) That is pure madness. It should be the other way around: *the primary task is to secure what is socially correct!*" [emphasis added] Crimes "against the People," such as the illegal crossing of internal zones or borders, were severely punished. There would be a trial in a courtroom, but the public "defender" would usually request a higher penalty for "these enemies of the People" than the prosecutor.

Who were these people in uniform? Who were the prosecutors, the judges, the bureaucrats, the informers, the new "teachers"? Together, they constituted the upper regions of what might best be described as the "upside-down" society. Often, those who ended up at the top had failed in their original careers. Once in control, the new leaders surrounded themselves with multiple layers of loyal-to-the-party nonachievers, recruited from the bottom of every profession. Upward mobility for the talented, for the real achievers, was first impeded, then stifled altogether. The new ruling class, like a concrete lid, inhibited everyone else (everyone who had not fled the country) from rising. They were the privileged few who always got first choice. They showed their gratitude by rendering unconditional service to the Cause. There was no need to whip them into line: Alone the regime ensured their position of privilege.

While Nazi Germany did not remain in existence long enough to slide into irreversible peacetime decline, the history of the Soviet Union and its satellites provides ample proof of the atrophy that sets in as socialism takes root. With the elimination of mobility in any direction, incentive, soon hope, disappeared. The ultimate irony was that, in theoretical writings, these regimes derided the lack of incentives in previous societies and promised gratification "in the future." Alas, people signed on to the premise, and assisted diligently in implementing their own demise until it became too late to change course.

This was the world for those living in the extreme manifestations of Franco-Germanic political thought; of the search for social justice; of the quest for the perfect society.

This was the world in which group identities, files, informers, and political officers determined a person's fate.

This was the world of the Commissar.

CHAPTER SIXTEEN

THE COMMISSARS
OF AMERICA

A DIFFERENT STRATEGY

How then does Franco-Germanic political thought affect present-day America?

Unlike the United States, neither Russia nor Germany could draw upon a tradition of successful political institutions. Before Lenin and Hitler came into power, Russians and Germans were both in the grip of major crises brought on by lost wars, hyperinflation, unemployment, and growing civil unrest.

Serious efforts were made in the 1960s to duplicate those conditions in America.

These efforts went on for a decade but with only limited success, because America's reserves in material wealth, in spiritual health, and in the love and practice of freedom were greater than any nation had ever possessed. Thus, the multiple attempts at outright revolution in the late 1960s failed. The attempt to engineer a major constitutional crisis through Watergate failed. The attempt at mortally wounding the American car industry (the touchstone of American manufacturing) through gasoline shortages and consumer hysteria failed. Consequently, Lenin's "Salami Tactic," renamed "incrementalism," seemed the only way. If America could not be dismantled, it needed to be transformed so as to remove the primary obstruction to the dominance of Franco-Germanic political doctrines.

The proposition that a society with America's record of success "ought to" alter course was preposterous, of course, and should have proved a near-impossible task. But the evidence shows otherwise; it is succeeding, however slowly, and it ought to be causing alarm. The slow speed of the transformation is due to America's reserves of strength. It is also the prudent course for those committed to it, as illustrated by the proverbial frog that was to be cooked alive. If thrown in boiling water, the animal mustered the energy to jump out. If placed in cold water, to be heated very slowly, the frog swam around enjoying a sense of well-being, and ended up cooked without further resistance.

Germany, although constituted with a legislative body, could muster neither institutional nor individual resistance when the new national socialist regime, on March 24, 1933, enacted the first Article of the Third Reich:

> In addition to the procedure outlined for the passage of legislation in the Constitution, the Federal Government [read: Executive Branch] is also authorized to pass laws.

In the United States, a change of this magnitude would have required a constitutional amendment—a lengthy process. But American advocates of such a change had neither the taste for a constitutional battle nor the intellectual honesty to disclose their true intent. The procedure nonetheless was introduced and made part of the landscape, but through the back door. Federal regulations, federal courts, and a battery of enforcers laid down and implemented—and continue to lay down and implement—an ever-growing chimera of "laws that aren't." Successful execution of such a campaign required two major components: a *method* specifically suited to the terrain, and a *new type of person* who could be employed in the service of that method.

The terrain—the United States of America, that is—presented the greatest difficulty since its inhabitants tended to take their basic liberties, as articulated in the Constitution, seriously. While those liberties could be curtailed through dilution—and dilution began immediately through a steady stream of new frivolous "rights"—that still left most original rights in place. Emotive and frontal attacks, such as those being hurled at the Second Amendment (the right to bear arms), could not be launched against, say, the First Amendment. While true freedom of speech is being curtailed daily through "political correctness" and by being designated as "hate speech," retaining it on the books is useful in the struggle to transform America, allowing the media to practice biased reporting to their heart's content. A successful method had to be universally applicable.

WEAPONS OF CHOICE

Property was chosen as the method. Its confiscation, actual or threatened, turned out to be the means by which the federal government could punish citizens for exercising their rights under the Constitution, thereby discouraging the exercise of those rights. Property also proved the Achilles' heel through which courts could demonstrate their ability to bankrupt people who insisted on their freedom of choice, thereby discouraging the exercise of free choice. The double dividend was the general loosening of the vital bond between owner and property—an indispensable precondition of freedom—and the gradual introduction of *fear*, which acts as a self-perpetuating bridle on freedom.

To succeed, the method also required the new type of person— new to America—suggested earlier. This new type needed to be trained to subordinate everything to the task of transforming America and Americans, convinced that "the old America was unsatisfactory." Preferably, this new type ought also to be either uninterested or unsuccessful in traditional fields of endeavor, possibly even averse to productive work. Last but not least, this new type's mind needed to be fully occupied by "social issues," leaving little room for real knowledge of any kind. This new type of person would create a whole new layer of society with powers to enforce the new creed. This new type of person was raw material for what became the *Commissar*.

The basic job of a commissar in America is to extend or withdraw privilege, and thereby to control and alter the behavior of the people. The tools of the job are simple: to dispense money or to mete out punishment. The dispensation of money may take the form of opportunity leading to money. Punishment comes mostly through inflicting property damage—also achievable by denying the opportunity for future funds. Punishment may also take the form of personal humiliation, as in mandatory "sensitivity training"—an invention that originated in the Stalinist practice of "self-criticism" and one that further stifles freedom of speech.

Sensitivity training publicly subordinates people to the authority of others who, ordinarily, know less and have accomplished less than themselves. Such is in the nature of the "upside-down" society. Often, though not always, commissars tend to be persons of low intellectual standing who find uncommon pleasure in exercising authority over their betters. In turn, the latter learn to assume an increasingly subservient posture by having to bow to persons whose authority is purely political. From time immemorial, two types of persons have made the best commissars: those who feel that society owes them, and those who are inebriated by a sense of mission. The latter type is able to do even more harm, because such individuals tend to come across as "caring and compassionate."

WHO?

As time progressed, the creation of commissar positions in America acquired the dimensions of a growth industry. The avalanche began with affirmative action officers, equal opportunity officers, judicial inquiry officers, and civil rights divisions. These positions exist for the sole purpose of enforcing a political agenda—an occupation at odds with the very nature of America. Certain college and university departments—departments of education, of communications, of journalism, social studies, and urban planning—became the reliable producers of commissars. Law schools, too, began to churn out graduates trained to serve a specific political agenda, rather than jurisprudence.

Soon, entire government departments were created to function as *Commissariats*, such as the Department of Education, Health and Human Services, the Environmental Protection Agency, the Department of Energy, and the Department of Commerce. Several other federal agencies, such as the National Endowment for the Arts, and its sister outfit, for the Humanities, fall into the same category. All these agencies offer services people find useful, and employ many capable professionals along with commissars. But they are of the same cloth, for they provide a platform for commissars, lack constitutional legitimacy, and are virtually immune to citizen complaints.

Eventually, commissar types found their way into legislatures, the Supreme Court, and the White House. The recent acquisition of the Department of Justice as a commissariat, and the growing multitude of commissar judges on federal benches, complete this massive force whose effectiveness—unlike the armies and submarines of the Third Reich or the ICBMs of the Soviet Union—has proved a match for America's awesome industrial, financial, and spiritual strength.

How to account for ordinary Americans who, in the millions, seem to be willing participants in the dismantling of their own country? To answer this, we have to go back to the 1960s one more time. As we observed, in Europe, the intellectual alliance of former fascists, national socialists, some social democrats, anarchists, Soviet-style and Western-style communists—now all gathered under an all-purpose Marxist umbrella—at last mustered the kinetic energy to launch their ideological missile across the Atlantic. As we also observed, by that time America offered a constituency eager to perform the docking maneuver on its arrival. An entire generation of Americans was affected, a generation now at the zenith of power. And here a point of seminal importance: *Unless a person has consciously repudiated the teaching of the 1960s, that person will unconsciously carry on the 1960s agenda.*

HOW?

Part of that agenda was the repudiation of the work ethic. "Before Woodstock," America had been the place where children of the affluent sold papers and mowed lawns to earn their pocket money. No more. The existence of commissars depends on society's acceptance of replacing community support for the needy with impersonal taxpayer support for people who do not perform useful work. Community support, of course, places certain obligations upon recipients because their lifestyle is visible to the community. Federal assistance is delivered "blind" because social workers dispense other people's money. And that is where commissar meets welfare recipient. The extent of the transformation is best illustrated by the enormous growth of the welfare recipient/social worker pool, in which two persons, neither of whom engages in productive work, perpetuate one another at the expense of those who do.

Repudiation of the work ethic totally transforms people's relationship to property. A growing multitude of persons who receive property in the form of grants and entitlements, or as salary for make-believe jobs, go through life without ever experiencing the thrill of real ownership. Their example exerts a highly corrupting effect on all others, placing in doubt—even disdaining—the value of effort. *By separating reward from effort, which ultimately separates effect from cause, Franco-Germanic political thought and its institutions (such as commissars) end up devastating the societies that adopt them.*

(There appears to be a contradiction between the strong work ethic German people have traditionally exhibited, and Franco-Germanic political philosophy which results in the destruction of that same quality. It will help to recall that the history of Germany contains many more contradictions.)

As we approach the end of the present millennium, the rule of the commissar covers the full range of human activity, from cradle to grave. Because it evolved from a way of political thinking, as opposed to an announced public policy, most of us have underestimated—or failed to notice—the network that surrounds us. Their numbers grow, because commissars invariably produce more commissars by looking for likely candidates, and by creating new areas for commissar authority. In addition, by now the network includes countless millions of volunteer "deputies." The growth in the number of self-appointed "commissar deputies" began when most of the education establishment, the media, and the entertainment industry signed on. Countless single-issue organizations sprang up to provide platforms for additional millions. Resistance to commissar rule was greatly reduced by sugarcoating every act of coercion with a certain merit, and surrounding it with righteous rhetoric. The spread of fear did the rest: individuals and corporations alike learned their lessons, the price of resistance, sooner or later.

WHERE?

The following is only one illustration of our current state. (A comprehensive survey would require volumes.) If not before, children are delivered to the commissar system when they enter public school. Here they are drilled to relate to one another in ways determined by the political agenda. Awareness of group identity; focus on group relationships, past and present; and treatment of the other sex (renamed "gender") are strictly enforced. The development of natural relationships between boys and girls is disrupted, while an almost perverted obsession with sex is manifested in the forced, premature discussion of sexual relations, and the distribution of condoms. Less and less is taught in the way of knowledge; more and more is geared toward the orthodox Marxist model called "school-to-work," which predetermines a child's future place in a regimented society. (The Clinton administration's successful campaign for "School to Work" started life in Marx's *Communist Manifesto*, where it is listed as No. 10 among the essential steps.) Parents learn early that the price of interfering with school-based commissars invites the attention of other commissariats, ranging from the "social services" all the way to the courts. And, through taxation, parents have to pay for these political incubators that masquerade as public schools, leaving them little with which to purchase a real education for their children.

If the student makes it to college or university, a commissar stands guard in the affirmative action office to administer the ongoing political agenda. For those students whose political preparation in high school was "incomplete," a battery of professional political operatives on the faculty and staff—outright Marxist-Leninists, feminists, gay-lesbian activists, African-American and Hispanic activists, officers for affirmative action, equal opportunity, and judicial inquiry—ensure that they do not "stray from the reservation." This is as alien to the idea of a university as commissariat-type government agencies to the idea of America.

The unavoidable byproduct of the foregoing survey is the risk of insulting any number of decent, honest, hard-working Americans who have stumbled into certain occupations and are trying to do a good job. Unfortunately, the participation of honorable persons does not alleviate the damage to society addressed on these pages.

And there is more. As if to make certain nothing is overlooked, speech codes are imposed and political discussions restricted to topics and viewpoints that are compatible with Franco-Germanic doctrine. The thoroughness of training is illustrated by the paucity of outside speakers who respect America's founding principles, and by the extreme hostility that greets them when they do appear. The success of the training is illustrated by the recent freeing up of campus-based commissars to expand their mission into "diversity training" (read: Franco-Germanic political indoctrination) for managers of corporations, signaling that their job inside Academia has been largely accomplished.

PAYING THE COST

Since neither free speech nor freedom of association has been officially suspended, the Department of Education in Washington uses property to restrict those rights. First, a large share of the taxpayers' property is requisitioned in the form of budget appropriations. Should any legislator attempt to resist, the price is public ridicule, and humiliation in the media. Few legislators will continue to resist once they have been portrayed as "enemies of education who want to keep disadvantaged children forever deprived of a fair opportunity." The money then is used to force all recipient institutions to abide by the political agenda. Institutions come to depend on federal funds, partly because of the cost of having to operate a growing number of bogus departments, such as Women's Studies, Hispanic Studies, African-American Studies, and partly because federal funding has an inflationary effect on tuition fees.

A word about "bogus departments." If female, black, and Hispanic contributions have been under-represented in the teaching of various disciplines, the remedy is to incorporate the relevant information in standard courses of study. That is where they belong. These segregated departments, just like the political operatives in the administration, have little to do with the role of a university. Their course of study is not built around a body of knowledge, but is a random collection of real and imaginary complaints against nature, the past, and society in general. More often than not, they offer a home both to faculty and students who would not otherwise find places in an institute of higher education. They also disseminate bogus information.

A wider array of commissar tools is available at the workplace. Personnel offices have been renamed "Human Resources" in an act of true *Gleichschaltung*. Instead of being persons, people have become a resource, along with animal, vegetable, and mineral resources. Generally, Human Resources is where the resident commissar sits. And there are three more awesome developments: One is a maze of regulations enforced by the Department of Labor, which supplant negotiated agreements and raise significantly the cost of hiring employees. Another is the proclivity of the courts to assess lethal amounts of monetary damages against entrepreneurs for frivolous reasons, like spilling hot coffee on one's lap. Last is the federal system of awarding contracts to high bidders if they are black, Hispanic, or female, thereby not only depriving persons of property—in this case the opportunity to earn a living—but also disrupting the entire structure of values. Reward is no longer given for effort; effect is separated from cause.

These are instances of commissar activity, of applying various aspects of "social justice." Since most of these practices fly in the face of America's founding principles, they tend to have at least one popular ingredient that will inhibit those who dare argue. For example: sex education can be beneficial—think of venereal disease—and surely passing out condoms is preferable to unwanted babies being drowned in lavatories. Certainly, the workplace ought to have reasonable safety precautions. And on and on.

FEAR, AGAIN

But the tragic result of it all has been transplanted directly from the Third Reich and the Soviet Union: *Americans have been taught to be afraid of one another.* Women are afraid of men because "all men are potential rapists." Men are afraid of women because sexual harassment charges hang over their every word and action. If the law permits, the most open-minded employer will stay away from "protected minorities" because all too often lawsuits take the place of honest work. Worst of all, parents and teachers are afraid of children. Perhaps nothing points to the totalitarian origins of America's so-called "liberals" as glaringly as their shameless use—abuse, rather—of children as the front behind which they operate.

Two memories stand out. The first goes back to the time when my class of twelve-year-olds was commandeered to march past and salute Stalin's new local representative as the newsreel cameras were rolling. The other was reading about third-graders marched out on the streets of Los Angeles carrying placards against items on the California ballot they could not possibly comprehend. Nowadays, every scheme politicians peddle is being proposed "for our kids." Children have been discovered as the resistance-proof access to other people's money, as demonstrated once again by President Clinton's January 1998 announcement to spend $21 billion on "childcare." Not surprisingly, the plan foresees further interference with traditional family life as well.

Can we assume, at least, that our children are content? The young contorted faces in movies, TV plays, or during interviews reveal alienated spirits. Children rant and rave about "solving the world's problems," while unable to read or write—or find on the map—the names of places whose problems they are proposing to solve. The commissars have stolen the childhood of our children, and their future as well.

In a recent move, not surprisingly, commissars have been appointed to organize and supervise what President Clinton designated as the "voluntarism project." Corporations are being told what amounts of money they must contribute "voluntarily," in order to pay those who "volunteer" their time. Not yet clear are the penalties, should someone fail to volunteer. While we contemplate the options, here is an old joke.

Truman, Churchill, and Stalin meet for the third time to sort out their differences. Again, no progress. After two frustrating days, Stalin says, "Comrades! We know that cats hate mustard. Whoever can induce a cat to eat some mustard will have his way." Challenge accepted. Truman, ever the straight shooter, takes the cat, takes a jar of mustard, and pours the latter into the mouth of the former. The cats spits out every last drop. Churchill, having watched this fiasco, prepares a sumptuous plate of liver, fish, and other cat's delights, with the tiniest drop of mustard in the center. The cat licks clean the entire plate—until he gets to the drop of mustard in the center. Stalin shakes his head with mock sympathy. "You have no idea how to do this," he says to the others. "Bring me a pound of mustard and watch!" With that, Stalin takes the mustard and smears all of it over the rear end of the cat. The animal frantically chases its tail and licks the area clean to the last drop.

A triumphant Stalin exclaims: "And, as you see, he did it *of his own free will*!"

CHAPTER SEVENTEEN

PEOPLE, WORDS, AND ATTITUDES

"OPPONENTS" OR "ENEMIES"?

American traditions of political discourse range from the rough-and-tumble to the noble and polished. On average, however, it is fair to say that the closer to the top, the higher the degree of civility and temperance. That state of affairs, like much else, is a matter of the past. One early consequence of commissar mentality has been the venomous tone that has become standard—both among politicians and in the media. Along with all the other manifestations of Franco-Germanic political philosophy and practice imported to America came changes in the relationship between political opponents. True to their tradition, those infected with the "virus" now look upon opponents as enemies. It was touching to watch the 1996 Republican nominee for president, Senator Bob Dole, insist again and again: "Bill Clinton is my opponent, not my enemy!" Many Democrats, ever since their party became home to those who wish to eviscerate America's heritage, have looked upon Republicans as the enemy.

To be sure, such is not the tradition of the Democratic Party, and some of its U.S. senators still make credible attempts to attend to the nation's business as statesmen who agree to disagree. But, by and large, Democrats have adopted the Franco-Germanic stance of belligerence.

Would-be commissars exist, and have always existed, everywhere. In America, the rule of law, the rights of individuals, the guarantee of property, and the natural regulatory capacity of free competition tended to restrict such persons to a small sphere of influence, and for a relatively short time. A school principal, a corporate CEO, a sheriff—even the governor of a state—may have succeeded in terrorizing the people under his authority, but not for long. People were able to help themselves. There were tools called the "law," and the law was with the people. If all else failed, a person could always move to the next town, the next county, another state.

THE "PEOPLE" FACTOR

Most of the time, of course, the need for desperate acts did not arise. One of the great mysteries of America has been the beneficial effect it has upon newcomers. A brief review of history tells of the bad ways people have treated one another in most places. Every other night, television serves up reminders of the wanton cruelty inflicted upon American prisoners of war by their Japanese, German, Korean, Iraqi, or Vietnamese captors. Treatment of that kind is not reserved for foreign captives: many natives of those, and of most other lands, have suffered the same. Yet when people from those same countries come to America, for the most part, they turn into peaceful Americans who coexist peacefully with other Americans. Since the make-up of these people is the same, America's societal arrangements must account for the beneficial change. Alas, as we now see, the process also works in reverse. Once in possession of powers that were never intended for government appointees, people's worst attributes have come to the fore. The "upside-down society" not only hoists the least worthy to the top, it also gives free rein to an individual's more sinister inclinations.

By definition, we expect judges to rise above petty personal pre-occupations. But recently, appointments, all the way to the U.S. Supreme Court, have been of people who seem to have a score to settle with society. A prime example is Associate Justice of the Supreme Court Ruth Bader Ginsburg, whose embittered feminism—of which she speaks openly—raises questions about her ability to rise above it.

By definition, we expect to find genuine civil servants in government departments, persons aware of their obligation to *serve* the people—*all* the people. Instead, we find persons like Norma V. Cantú, Assistant Secretary in the U.S. Department of Education, whose recent public statements about the California ballot initiative, and actions related to it, confirm her contempt for the will of the people.

By definition, we expect modesty, and the highest ethical standards of those entrusted with the highest office. Instead, elementary rules of personal and official conduct are flaunted daily. The *Wall Street Journal* reported in January 1998 that the U.S. Department of Justice holds low-level federal employees to a higher standard than it does the president or the vice president of the United States.

That is the human profile, the nature of the world which is ruled increasingly by commissars.

LETHAL WEAPONS I—WORDS

The word "fair" has suddenly appeared on every lip. "Fairness" is demanded by all. The trouble is, the original meaning of the word has undergone a complete transformation. "Fair play" used to stand for an attitude of *self*-restraint. A "fair" person would not take "unfair" advantage of the weaker position of another person. Until recently, it has been a matter of individual choice to act in a "fair" or "unfair" manner.

In contemporary usage, however, it is for persons or groups to announce whether, in their opinion, they have been fairly or unfairly treated. "Unfair" treatment may have been inflicted by someone alive or long dead, by nature, or by fate. In any event, what used to be a virtue to be admired has become a hammer with which to hit other people over the head. Once persons declare that they have been the subject of "unfairness," they become "entitled" to some form of compensation. And it is up to a commissar to administer the new entitlement.

"Entitlement" is another word tool whose long-term damage cannot be measured in dollars. The long-term damage is the addition of the word to our daily vocabulary, the state of inertia it inflicts upon all, and the disease it spreads in every nook of society. The industrious will be less so, because the fruits of effort are confiscated; the lazy will be more so because money is being delivered to them by the post office. The record shows that every entitlement leads to additional entitlements, and that successive generations soon begin to speak of them as "rights." People today proclaim that those who lack the means to provide for themselves nevertheless have a "right" to good health, a "right" to good housing, a "right" to higher education. Once talk of such rights is accepted as legitimate, the corresponding obligation upon the productive members of society is accepted along with it. And if the productive members of society balk, their attitudes—their behavior— must be altered. Representative Jesse Jackson Jr. of Illinois proclaimed repeatedly on national televison that "it is the role of government to change the behavior of the people." Not to be outdone, President Clinton announced in September 1997 that he was "going to change the behavior of the people." ("The philosophers have only interpreted the world. The point is to change it."—Karl Marx)

THE "GOOD" AND THE "EVIL"

Such statements divide the citizens of this country into two groups at least. The majority needs its behavior changed; a minority has identified the need and is taking steps to effect the change. That was hardly the intention at the time the Preamble to the Constitution was written. Its opening phrase, "We The People," implied a single conglomeration of humans, and served instant notice of the citizens' authority to determine the behavior of government—not the other way around.

But "We The People" does not fit into the Franco-Germanic worldview. At the very least, there must be two opposing groups resulting from a pair of key words: oppression and exploitation. Without these words, commissars would have to pack up and go home. "Oppression" presumes the existence of oppressors and oppressed. "Exploitation" presumes the existence of exploiters and exploited. Commissars are appointed to punish oppressors and exploiters, and to assign privileges to the oppressed and exploited. In America, this has been expanded to include descendants of the formerly oppressed and exploited.

This is not to deny the tendency of the strong to oppress, exploit, and otherwise take advantage of the weak. But all such acts are inflicted by a person upon another person. The corruption of these words occurs when it is asserted that a group oppresses and exploits another group. These conditions, commissars argue, are not responsive to individual relief such as may be offered by a court of law functioning in the American tradition. Commissars are needed to rein in the offenders and compensate the victims.

It is also a fundamental tenet of Franco-Germanic political thought that group characteristics do not change: once an oppressor, always an oppressor. Once an exploiter, always an exploiter. And the number of victims keeps growing—hence the need for ever more commissars; hence the growing intensity in the rhetoric; hence the absurd conditions under which the offspring of a black millionaire, or of a Spaniard who may have helped to wipe out the Incas, will be favored over America's pioneers, or refugees from one of Europe's tyrannies.

A division of society into "good" and "evil" is reflected also in the recent proliferation of the term "working Americans." Implied is the existence of segments in our society who "do not work." That was how the Third Reich portrayed Jews; that was how the Soviet Union branded everyone who owned property. Who are the targets in America? (Certainly not those who live on welfare.)

LETHAL WEAPONS II—STATISTICS

Commissars also rely heavily on statistics. Commissariats were originally created because "society is unable or unwilling to reform itself." Statistics are rolled out to support statements of this kind. Logic would dictate steady improvement once the commissars have had the opportunity to coerce "reluctant" people to adopt desirable behavior patterns. But as we know, such is not the case. Statistics reveal steadily worsening conditions, deepening the fault lines that separate the groups into which American society has been successfully splintered. Every day, we are admonished, the gulf separating "the affluent" and "the needy" grows wider. Every year, the academic standing of public schools sinks to new lows, causing the crisis in education to reach new highs. Whether it is the homeless, the drug-addicted, or the disabled, the numbers keep rising. Add up the total percentages of all officially "disadvantaged" groups—women, blacks, Hispanics, disabled, sexually different—and it comes to more than 100 percent. Add up the numbers of all who claim to suffer from one illness or another, and it seems that there are no healthy people anywhere from sea to shining sea. While this may sound facetious, Franco-Germanic political doctrines—advocates of social justice, "liberals"—are truly as unrealistic as that.

LETHAL WEAPON III—BRANDING

"Branding" provides the means to make certain that no one dares argue with corrupted words and phony statistics. The current, constantly expanding roster of brandings ranges from "cold-hearted," through "mean-spirited," "sexist," "homophobic," all the way to "racist." Several important characteristics should be noted. First, those who have been classified as "oppressed" or "exploited" are unconditionally exempt from branding. Second, the idea and practice was developed in Nazi Germany and Soviet Russia, where "Jew-friendly," "class-alien," and similar brandings instantly declared open season on anyone so designated. And last but not least, branding prepares society for the gradual introduction of political "crime"—integral to commissar rule.

The concept of political crime is utterly alien to Anglo-American political thought. Indeed, nothing illustrates better the chasm separating Franco-Germanic from Anglo-American political institutions. The former cannot operate without, and the latter is inconceivable with. The incompatibility of political crimes with the U.S. Constitution is unequivocal. By definition, political "crimes" take the form of speech, publication, association, or assembly, not held to be desirable by the government of the day. A society with our Bill of Rights does not permit government even to say, much less dictate, what is desirable. The acquiescence of American society in the aggressive use of branding has paved the way to a kind of halfway house, leading to the official establishment of political crimes—a move which would effectively invalidate the U.S. Constitution. The halfway house bears the label "hate crime."

Like so much else, "hate crime" has been slipped into the national consciousness without resistance. It is posited that if a white person injures a black person, a "hate crime" has been committed. But just as it was suggested earlier that "acts of conscience" are not enhanced by the qualifier "social," so the culpability of a "crime" does not depend on sentiment. Our laws have always called for the punishment of those who inflict harm on others, regardless of motive.

But, motive there is—and a crucial one at that—in the minds of those who have introduced the concept of hate crime. For starters, it promotes and solidifies the divisions of society. Those to whom commissars give victim status cannot be accused of hate crimes, just as they are free from branding. But such favored persons must be practicing victims. Those who choose not to accept victim status— blacks who are simply American, women at peace with themselves, homosexuals who won't act up, Hispanics who desperately want to learn English—are automatically grouped with oppressor/exploiters who, of course, are forever vulnerable to a charge of hate crime. This latter group is also under constant suspicion of engaging in "hate speech." Hate speech is treated similarly to what we called "branding" because it may be freely practiced by persons enjoying victim status, as well as by members of the commissar class—regardless of sex, skin tone, religion, or ethnic origin.

Few indicators of the transformation of our society are as alarming as our acquiescence that certain crimes, by definition, can be committed only by persons of a certain type.

TOWARD CONDITIONAL OWNERSHIP

And now back to the question of property, but from a different, significantly broader perspective. The new levels of administrative power, the new array of punitive tools, have changed our relationship to property. Oppressors/exploiters are not really entitled (there is that word again) to theirs. Behind many a crime statistic lies not so much the depravity of the criminal, but the insinuation that those who are not designated victims are most likely the beneficiaries of "ill-gotten gains." As yet class warfare has not resulted in actual changes in the Constitution. But both commissars and designated victims have placed property rights permanently in their cross-hairs: commissars because they understand that freedom is a function of guaranteed property; "victims" because it is easier to take than to earn. The joke is on today's privileged "victims." If history serves as a warning, commissars give certain groups the advantage only so long as it enhances the commissars' authority. The assumption that commissars actually "like" anyone has been the costliest deception of the twentieth century.

Meanwhile, the ground has been prepared: Americans no longer feel secure in their property. Those who have acquired it legitimately are being taught that there is a price to be paid for keeping it, and that they do so at the commissars' pleasure. Those who are simply given it are learning that the hand that giveth, just as easily taketh away. Don't forget the allegory of the slowly cooking frog. As of now, we tend not to be unduly concerned because, except in the form of taxation, relatively little private property has been officially requisitioned by government to date.

But then, the terms of the game have changed beyond recognition.

CHAPTER EIGHTEEN

COMMUNISM COMES OF AGE

RESTORING THE WORDS

As efforts to change the meaning of conventional words (fairness, work, rights) progressed, the use of certain other words (socialist, communist), judged to be inimicable to the agenda, were restricted. Amazingly, this was met with yet more acquiescence. Thus, people who are painfully aware of massive, unwelcome changes in the American reality, and who know perfectly well the direction of those changes, seem paralyzed when it comes to calling them by name. That, in turn, has fostered mistaken assumptions with regard to available remedies. Foremost among these is the obsession with "big government." Concern with the size of government falls in the same category as an undiagnosed tumor. Is it just a swelling, a cyst—or is it cancer? Our bloated government is merely the symptom. The size would shrink naturally once we found the strength to do away with the functions it currently usurps, and restore an attitude of service.

We might begin by restoring meaning to the words we use. Once again, we ought to focus on what communism aims to accomplish at the end of the day—"social justice"—not the examples of its adolescence, of its "Sturm und Drang." Every communist (and socialist, and national socialist, and liberal, and even social democrat) will concede: "Mistakes were made. They must be corrected." What this amounts to is the assurance, "Next time it will work."

Recall that Lenin called leftist thinking an "infantile disorder" of communism. By the same token, the wholesale nationalization of property and the murder of tens of millions were most likely convulsions of adolescence. The dismantling of the Soviet Union, that ultimate act of self-criticism, ought to persuade even the most skeptical among us that communism has grown up. Communism has become mature and wise. Communism is ready for the big time.

Communism is ready for America.

ERRORS OF ADOLESCENCE

Along the way, three big mistakes were made. First was the costly error of killing millions of people. Next in importance was the confiscation of the means of production. Finally, it proved counterproductive to maintain power through a monolithic party, and to continue calling it "communist."

The first of these errors had its origins in the French Revolution of 1789. Mass killing had occurred before, of course, but the spectacle of the state, "in the name of the people," engaging in the public execution of entire categories of people was new. It introduced the concept of administrative extermination. Even the Spanish Inquisition offered the opportunity of repentance. There is no way out if the "crime" is based on an accident of birth.

And so, Lenin, Stalin, and Hitler took their cue from Danton and Robespierre. In their zeal, they overlooked the harm inflicted upon their own cause. The people they killed happened to be among the most productive, ordinarily considered as assets to a nation. Harvesting the possessions of millions of Jews was obviously tempting, but the benefits proved short-lived. Harnessing their creative powers could have given Hitler lasting advantages. Similarly, the kulaks, the Ukrainians, the shopkeepers who were killed on orders from Lenin and Stalin may have yielded up their land and possessions. But the Soviet Union permanently lost those who knew how to make the land produce food, and how to get it to the people. Russia has not been able to feed itself since.

The second error occurred when German methodology was married to French egalitarianism, as in the writings of Marx. For obscure reasons, even detractors of Marx credit his "great contributions" to economics. My generation received theoretical training in Marxism— and experienced the starvation that inevitably follows when it is applied. Marx prescribed taking into "public" ownership all means of production. That doctrine proved a disaster wherever consummated. State bureaucracies are utterly unable to manage economies. But the error should have been obvious to Marx himself. For it was none other than Karl Marx who explained the failure of all previous economic systems as *the failure to ensure that all participants in the process of production have a vested interest in its outcome*. The same Karl Marx then prescribed a recipe that made certain that *no participant* in the process of production had a vested interest in the outcome.

The third error was Russian in origin, contributed by Vladimir Ilyich Lenin. Russia had never progressed beyond a feudal hierarchy, and the strict orthodoxy of the Eastern Church was successful in attracting an unwavering allegiance by its members. Lenin thus took the view that only a similarly feudal structure and an alternative orthodoxy could compete successfully with the existing order. Hence he built a party hierarchy much along the lines of the Church, and made the party's infallibility an article of religious canon. From 1919 onward, Leninist parties everywhere copied the ecclesiastic structure, while writers and artists created an equally religious universe around the word "communist." Novels and short stories about conversion reached epiphany when the hero joined the party. The halo that once adorned saints was spread over the Kremlin at the close of motion pictures. Hitler, too, made himself into an object of religious worship, and the Nuremberg rallies replaced the pilgrimages of old, where revelation awaited the faithful.

LESSONS LEARNED

Both the religious organization of the party, and continued use of the "communist" label required that people be kept uninformed—a Russian tradition of long standing. But with the breathtaking development in communications, a label tainted with the blood of millions, and a hierarchy long since declared inefficient, the party could not (and did not) survive. Practically no one is a "communist" today. What happened? Fundamental attitudes don't disappear into thin air. People might die, but ideas rarely do, *especially when the idea is one of only two major strains of political thought that excite the people, dominate the minds, and determine the affairs of man for centuries.*

The more credible assumption is that the lessons have been understood and learned. Certainly, when it comes to the third "error," there is every appearance of success. The labels—communist, socialist—have gone altogether. If anyone attempts to use them, a chorus of protest is unleashed: "Are you looking for reds under every bed?" And, "The Wall is down; what more do you want?" Then follows the branding "redbaiter" or "redbasher." But most don't even try. The only "old" label retained comes from Stalin's clever deception—calling German national socialists "fascists." Today's communists and their dupes tend to call everyone they don't like a "fascist."

It must count among the most amazing spectacles of history to be inundated with the rhetoric, theory, and practice of communism, and see not one communist around. We read and hear daily about class warfare, redistribution of wealth, the "dispossessed" masses, the disadvantaged, universal health care, speech codes, sensitivity training, restrictions on parents' rights, school-to-work—the list goes on and on. The agenda is with us, the Party is not.

THE NETWORK OF NO NAME

But the "communist" label is not the only thing that has disappeared. The impracticality of a monolithic party organization has also been learned. Creating a network of single-issue enthusiasts is not only easier, but very American. People tend to be passionate about one thing, *their* thing. The job is then to persuade people that other causes are a logical match, and that mutual support will yield mutual benefits.

Thus, protectors of, say, the baby seal will team up with those who oppose nuclear tests which, after all, might kill the baby seal's parents. Advocates of nuclear weapons are most likely military "hawks," whose wars are always fought on the backs of the dispossessed who, in America, are first and foremost black. Black people have difficulty obtaining a good education because of wealthy white men who control the school curriculum and skew tests to favor their offspring. Many of them make their ill-gotten profits by land speculation, displacing small helpless animals and birds that lived there millions of years before any humans appeared. These land developers ring up extra profits by employing cheap labor, mostly women, who are paid less than men for the same work. Or they hire undocumented aliens who are enticed to come here, only to be denied the most elementary human rights to education and health care. The least we can do for the children of these hardworking newcomers is to let them take classes in their own language. We have forgotten, but they, like our own Native Americans, can teach us how to live in peace with nature, save the rain forest—and protect the baby seal. [Applause. Pause for breath.]

Add to this the entire gamut of the environmental movement, and Lenin must be green (no pun intended) with envy at the sight of such a self-sustaining organization. It requires low maintenance, yet offers high dependability because people support that which comes to them naturally.

ALTERNATIVES CONSIDERED

As for the killings, even the Chinese communists have begun to abandon the idea. The minor massacre at Tiananmen Square is to the Cultural Revolution of 1966 as a nose bleed is to the amputation of all four limbs. But why kill people when you can make them work for you? The overwhelming majority of those killed in the Third Reich and in the Soviet Empire would gladly have worked in exchange for their lives.

Clear, too, are the lessons of the second error—taking all means of production into "public" ownership—which led to economic disaster in each and every case. (Mussolini, the seasoned socialist, and Hitler may have sensed the inherent inefficiency of the proposition and decided not to adopt this particular doctrine of Franco-Germanic political thought.) For the most part, Marxist economics were introduced in poor countries with little or no industrial base. But even in highly industrialized Great Britain, where nationalization of industries was adopted after World War II, the results were dismal. Reprivatization saved Britain from terminal bankruptcy.

All these lessons have been learned and absorbed into the latest, mature, brilliantly reconstituted incarnation of communism, which is busily building the bridge to the twenty-first century, to the third millennium, and social justice.

THE REALLY "NEW ECONOMIC POLICY"

The appetite to manage all corporations, large and small, has given way to the realization that a combination of threats, restrictions, and controls will provide access to the fruit, without ever having to plant the tree, buy the fertilizer, or perform any of the ongoing chores that go with production. Dead cows, or those made of clay, cannot be milked, and dead geese do not lay eggs, golden or otherwise.

The next important shift occurred when it was realized that, in America, the engines of liberty were not the large corporations—primary targets of classical communist attention—but the small entrepreneurs. The guarantee of freedom in America has been everyone's ability to escape the constraints that both managements of large corporations and labor unions impose upon individual prerogative. The *availability* of choice was always there. And that availability was predicated on the guarantee of property and the freedom to enter into contract.

The dilemma was how to bring about a gradual curtailment of that freedom—both in the marketplace and in people's personal affairs—while *harnessing the profits of a free-market economy* to build communism. Communism—or social justice—and freedom are incompatible. In the past, so were communism and free-market economies. But since only the free market can deliver the financial means necessary for the successful communization of society, solving the dilemma—"squaring the circle"—became a matter of survival.

The solution was the two-tiered approach seen in America today. Small business is being gradually choked by hostile regulations, mandatory procedures, and punitive taxation. Foremost is the suspension of the right to enter into contract with employees freely. The federal government has become a kind of "super" labor union, but with a difference: a union has to negotiate first; the government does not. A battery of commissars enforces edicts prescribing who must be employed, as well as the terms of the employment.

Small business must provide benefits it is less and less able to afford. By now, these include time off if a worker needs to take the family pet to the vet. Such an allowance may well be made by a sensible employer on a person-to-person basis. But in the move toward communism, even the smallest details of human conduct must be either forbidden, or else mandatory. In other words, people with commissar mentality derive advantage from the mere act of enforcing a regulation, as well as from the specific impact of such a regulation.

Americans tend to be fiercely independent. For this reason, many will do what it takes to start up or to continue in business. But the walls and the ceiling of their world are closing in, as Edgar Allan Poe depicts in *The Pit and the Pendulum*. Unless there is a reversal of policy, more and more will give up the uneven fight before they are squashed. That day is drawing nearer. On June 25, 1997, the White House released a memo ordering the *further* curtailment of federal contracts awarded to small businesses. Concurrently, Senate Minority Leader Tom Daschle, South Dakota Democrat, blocked a vote that would have permitted small businesses to combine for the purpose of bidding.

The strangulation of small business does not necessarily trouble the large corporations. Many of them swallow up smaller businesses themselves. Besides, large corporations have been learning and adapting themselves to the new rules of the game. The game is one of stick-and-carrot, rather than the outmoded concentration camp approach.

The stick has been demonstrated in a variety of ways. The larger the corporation, the more vulnerable it is to assaults on its name and reputation. Corporations have been accused of polluting the air and the water, of jacking up prices, of practicing discrimination, of deliberately selling harmful products. These charges have been leveled, and thus used as a tool, whether true or not. The trial—"trial by hysteria"—is conducted instantly and in public. Nowhere has the complicity of the scientific community—now funded largely by commissars—and the entertainment and news media proved of greater value than in their willingness to amplify any message the commissars wish to convey.

Large corporations must demonstrate their subservience to commissars and pay "protection" money. The grand example was made of the tobacco industry. Even paying a ransom running into the hundreds of billions has not brought a cessation of daily assaults on it. Then, from time to time selected groups are given leave to help themselves to the contents of corporate purses—oil companies being a favored target, as the cases of Texaco and Exxon demonstrate. Dow Chemical is another recent example: women, many of whom chose to avail themselves of breast implants, have been invited to dip into Dow's till.

MAKING AN EXAMPLE

The story of the tobacco industry demonstrates the *modus operandi*, and a number of collateral points. To begin with, scientific evidence is published, pointing to the existence of harmful consequences that are beyond dispute. That way the requisite popular element is secured. Then some "I-always-hated-the-stuff" people link up with activist types and demand the first official measures to "protect the public." Over many years, the frog gets cooked very, very slowly as we go from "no smoking" sections in airplanes and restaurants to the superbranding of smoking, *and smokers*, as "Public Enemy No. 1."

In reality, the antitobacco campaign has little if anything to do with health concerns, and everything to do with behavior control. It demonstrates to the citizen how individual behavior can and will be controlled, and it persuades corporations of the wisdom to pay up before their image is dragged through the gutter. Branding techniques reached unprecedented levels of sophistication: the *Washington Post*, in an August 1997 article about an entirely unconnected controversy, referred to Senator Jesse Helms of North Carolina as "(R-Tobacco)." And while cigarette smoking is attacked with the hysterical passion of a witch hunt, our fifth-graders continue to be heavily engaged in the use of narcotics with only an occasional expression of regret from government officials.

UPSIDE-DOWN LOGIC

In the world of the commissar, logic, too, is turned upside-down. Attorneys general of assorted states argue that smokers cost taxpayers a great deal of money through Medicare and Medicaid expenditures required for their treatment. The communization of Americans has advanced to such a level that no one exposes the nonsense by pointing out that the burden was placed on the taxpayer by *socialized* medicine, not by the smoker. We accept, also, the technique hitherto used only by the gambling community: a certain portion of the public's investment in corporations is skimmed off in a "civilized" manner, as in the case of the "voluntarism project," and it becomes the cost of doing business. Commissars have learned the wisdom of such an arrangement, as have most large corporations and the public. As in the casino world, no one gets "roughed up," and the "bosses" take care of security.

And, along with the stick comes the occasional carrot, of course. Recently, the president agreed to get tough with Japan on behalf of Federal Express, and the late Secretary of Commerce Ron Brown used to arrange all manner of foreign liaisons for "qualified" corporations, witness the joint ventures in China of Chrysler and Sprint.

But, if any doubt remained about the validity of the broad, long-term view taken here, such doubts were dispelled the day after the great tobacco settlement was announced. The media reported a meeting by scientists and activists to discuss the harmful effects of caffeine—and initial measures to regulate its use.

TIGHTENING THE NOOSE

Is it a coincidence that so many recent changes appear to weaken America, to divert its resources? Some answers might come from the recently enacted law known as the "Americans With Disabilities Act," or ADA. As with all such measures, it contains legitimate and desirable elements. If a society can afford it, people who are handicapped ought to be provided with opportunities to work, and with facilities to enjoy life. That, however, does not account for the manner in which ADA was placed on the agenda, or for many of its provisions.

Recently, I heard a speech given by Isabelle Katz Pinzler, assistant attorney general, Civil Rights Division, U.S. Department of Justice, entitled "The Americans With Disabilities Act as Common Sense." Ms. Katz Pinzler spoke variously about the forty-two million, forty-seven million, forty-nine million disabled Americans—the numbers appeared to grow with her passion about the topic—asserting, among other things, that their previous exclusion from life in America "had rendered this nation unable to compete in world markets." During the question-and-answer period, I asked her about the source of her figures, noting that it would seem unlikely that a full one-fifth of Americans would be disabled and had been, until recently, "excluded from our national life."

"Good question," Ms. Katz Pinzler exclaimed. "I have no idea where those numbers come from. Heather!" she asked someone at the back of the hall—"where *do* those numbers come from?" A voice came back timidly, "The Census Bureau, I guess."

A phone call to the Census Bureau revealed that in the mid-1980s, quiet instructions were passed around to start tabulating people with disabilities in preparation for the general survey of 1990. The answers to a simple question about disability were never to be corroborated. The Census Bureau worker at the other end seemed as perplexed as I was that no supporting evidence was required.

We then went on to the specific questions asked. One of them simply inquired if anything had been experienced during the past six months that had rendered the subject unable to perform tasks other people can in ordinary circumstances. Given the wording of the question, the surprise is not how high the percentage appears (currently just under 25 percent, or one-fourth of all men, women, and children), but how low. Certainly, most of us have experienced some moments when we were unable to perform tasks others could.

(A subsequent conversation with an actual census worker shed light on the method. Answers given by the subject are to be recorded, even if the physical evidence contradicts it. If a subject claims, say, that a dwelling consists of two rooms, two rooms have to be recorded even if three rooms are visible.)

The moral is: there is a constant search for a fresh supply of victims, as well as for statistics justifying "urgent action." By the time the ADA bill came before Congress, numbers had been created that, like most statistics currently in use, bore not the slightest semblance to reality. Relying on hysteria, the tool that never fails, ADA was packed with ridiculous requirements enforced in every nook and cranny of the land. Ultra-liberal Yale University almost closed its concert hall because it cost over a million dollars to create handicapped access to its upper, as well as to its ground, level.

ADA's insane requirements hit small business the hardest. The groundwork was also laid for a whole new batch of frivolous lawsuits—another diversion of national resources. And, of course, new ways were established for the redistribution of wealth. Small business had no power to resist, and big business had learned not to resist.

Commissar-power is best illustrated by what Ms. Katz Pinzler calls "common sense." At one point she said, "Why, if a business is located on the second floor and does not have the space to install a wheelchair-sized elevator, *I would give them permission* to construct a street-level counter instead, and serve the disabled there."

Even a few years ago, neither such an attitude nor such a statement by a public servant would have been feasible, much less acceptable, in America.

ENVIRONMENT

Environment comes last, because it is the most developed, the most insidious, and the broadest-based of all tools destructive to property—and thus, to freedom. None is more conducive to emotional divisiveness. None can more easily marshal concerted, international activism. Positively none has brought forward more pseudo-science, more hypocrisy, more hysteria, and more outright prevarication.

And none is predicated on more agreeable grounds. The *stated* objectives that undergird the "three angels of destruction"—the Clean Air Act, the Clean Water Act, and the Endangered Species Act—are, as usual, unimpeachable. All of us prefer to breathe fresh air, ingest and swim in pure water, and be protective of wildlife. The success with which these areas of natural agreement have been turned into the bloodiest of battlefields should warn us of the exceptional brilliance, tenacity, and determination of the opposite side.

Any consideration of the environmental weapon must begin with a reminder that America and Americans have led the world in designating, operating, and visiting a network of national parks. Americans have also been first in cleanliness: individual bathrooms in every hotel, deodorants, toothpaste, you name it.

Without a doubt, the exhaust fumes of cars and factories, the exponential growth in chemical waste brought on by the plastics revolution, the previously undetected harm caused by certain products—all required attention and appropriate remedies. Indeed, an honest, realistic, politically neutral environmental agenda could have united this nation as could no other initiative. Instead, from the outset, environmentalists have shown their true colors—and it has nothing to do with green. Their campaigns always hit targets in the classic communist tradition—industry, land ownership, and America's strength: freedom of choice.

Those are harsh words, but a look at the energy sector will prove the point. The oil companies have been under constant attack. Do environmentalists prefer clean nuclear power? No, of course not.

Nuclear power plants are "evil." That would leave coal but, during the 1996 campaign, President Clinton placed America's largest reserves of "clean" coal beyond reach by designating 1.7 million acres in Utah as the "Grand Staircase Escalante National Monument." "America's national interest" is a phrase that has yet to cross the lips of an American environmentalist.

A personal experience. In the 1991 elections in Bloomington, Indiana, the mayoral campaign revolved around an incinerator to do away with PCB dumps that Westinghouse Corporation had built up at a time when no one was aware of any possible harmful effects. For years, environmentalists had painted daily pictures about the effects of "killer PCBs," which gave rise to lawsuits filed by everyone who had worked around them. One day, touring the PCB dumps, my wife noticed that trees seemed to be particularly green around the sites, and a profusion of birds were flying about. Life appeared to thrive. That evening, I mentioned this to an engineer friend. He shook his head. "No one has proved as yet that PCBs are harmful, even if taken internally," he said with a chuckle. Slowly, word got around that fumes from the proposed incinerator would cause much more harm than the PCBs. A whole new campaign began and, after some more hysteria in the opposite direction, plans for the incinerator were dropped.

AL GORE AND AMERICAN INTERESTS

In most places, freedom of movement has remained but a dream for centuries. The automobile represents to Americans the ultimate freedom of movement. Since the first Model "T" rolled off the line, few have been dependent on the schedule of others, and both cars and fuel have been affordable. Of course, cars—and gas—would be even more affordable if environmentalists had not imposed crippling requirements on the industry.

But car travel is still more affordable in America than anywhere else and will remain so unless and until the likes of environmental activist Albert Gore Jr. have their way. Apparently unaware that his obsessions threaten our freedom to move about, he is eagerly promoting the myth about "global warming," for which there is not a shred of undisputed evidence. Observations over a few decades are obviously of no significance when it comes to long-term predictions about the properties of our planet. The embarrassing reality is that as yet we cannot foretell with any degree of certainty in which direction a hurricane will move over *the next twenty-four hours*. Undeterred, the person wishing to become president of the United States appears at global conferences with the intent further to restrict American industry. In this effort, he has harnessed scores of others who are unlikely to have America's best interests in mind. Presumably, Mr. Gore's rationale is that we are now part of some "global interest."

How? Unless the environmentalist movement has been appointed to speak for mankind, their demands appear to be merely a cover for the confiscation of property, the *de facto* repeal of property rights, and the curtailment of freedom.

"BY GOVERNMENT ACTION"

Stories of the commissars' actions abound, and Congress, at last, is showing some interest. California Representative Richard Pombo wrote an entire book (*This Land Is Our Land*), and Senator Orrin Hatch of Utah has introduced legislation about the need to protect property. Meanwhile, the assault on property has taken on the appearance of the nine-headed hydra. What began in the name of "pollution control" became the "preservation of animals," went on to protect vegetation, and ended up declaring that mud (called "wetlands") was our "sacred trust" upon which the survival of the planet depended. In the name of any of the above, people's property may be forfeited, left in possession but with its value decreased or eroded, productive work can be prohibited, and money confiscated either by executive penalty or lawsuits adjudicated by a commissar judge. The latter frequently award the money so confiscated to organizations that form part of the commissar network, such as the Sierra Club.

In western states, the federal government owns vast tracts of land, more than 80 percent in Nevada. A battery of agencies regulates those lands, gradually restricting their use by citizens. The tendency, demonstrated again and again by the current administration, is to force humans off the land altogether and to make it appear that human activity is "offensive to nature."

American interests always seem to end up on the losing side. A century of gold mining north of Yellowstone Park came to a sudden halt when the U.S. government reached an agreement with a Canadian company to cease activities. The Canadian company received $65 million from the American taxpayers, the states of Wyoming and Montana will lose about $233 million in revenues, and untold millions of the taxpayers' money will be expended to erase the scars on the land. If left alone, the Canadian company would have taken care of that.

Even when the federal government does not own the land, the means at its disposal to inflict harm are virtually unlimited. A snail, a rat, a bit of mud—anything will do for federal inspectors to impose any number of arbitrary restrictions. One of the most important traditions of the English-speaking world is that a search warrant or the owner's permission is required to enter the premises of a citizen, for his "home is his castle." These vital safeguards have become moot. "Environmental crimes" run a parallel course with "political crimes."

The roster of intrusions upon private property could fill several volumes. Here is one example. The federal Fish and Wildlife Service discovered that a pond belonging to a Mr. Child was "habitat" for the Kanab ambersnail. The area around the pond was fenced off, and neither the owner nor any other human was permitted nearby. Soon thereafter, some geese started camping out around the pond. First, the federal government instructed the Utah

Department of Wildlife to shoot the geese, cut open their stomachs, and bring the contents to Salt Lake City to see whether they had eaten some snails. If so, the government could fine the owner $50,000 for each snail. When the presence of news photographers deterred a federally sponsored slaughter of geese, the government of the United States, Protector of the Free World, induced vomiting in the geese to see if any snails would turn up. (None did.)

COMMISSAR NETWORK IN ACTION

These laws have been enacted with the help of well-meaning Americans and will continue to be used until enough of us accept the reality that the *radical transformation of America* is the intended outcome of the present conflict. In this conflict, the Franco-Germanic side is fully supported by a broad network of forces. No sooner did Senator Hatch come forward with his Omnibus Property Rights Act of 1997 than James Ryan, a "civil rights" attorney, and Douglas Kendall, organizer of an action group to combat property rights, unleashed a reinterpretation of the so-called Takings Clause in the Fifth Amendment of the Constitution. Because the Constitution is silent on the effect of environmental edicts on property, the men contended that property thus assailed was outside constitutional protection. But suddenly, in true commissar style, their analysis of the Constitution switched to branding those who disagreed with them by asserting that such persons were also opposed to anything "that benefits women, minorities, and other victims of prejudice."

Constant support, also, is provided by television networks, such as the Discovery Channel, which never misses an opportunity to chastise by calling humans "enemies of nature," or "the worst predators." This antihuman attitude parallels government actions that give precedence to wolves, grizzly bears, and mountain lions over human life. Occasionally, the big networks chime in as well. On July 19, 1996, NBC concluded its series *Virus* by declaring that the terrible virus hiding somewhere in the rain forest was not the greatest enemy of the planet—*Man* was. Added *Time* in August 1997: "It's humans, not sharks, who are nature's most fearsome predators." True to Franco-Germanic doctrine, viewers and readers, especially young ones, are conditioned to see nature as "good" and humans as "evil."

And, again, a personal experience. An elderly couple in Bloomington, Indiana, lived a long life on a piece of property which they kept in legendary condition for decades. Their families had been there so long that the street was named for them. Time came when they needed to sell the property because they had become physically unable to tend it. When environmentalists found out that the proposed purchaser needed to have two trees cut down, the entire community was incited against the elderly couple. Leading the hysteria was a woman whose front yard was known to resemble an abandoned garbage dump. It is a disturbing fact that many activists who campaign for clean air and clean water seem not to object to unclean persons, or neighborhoods that are covered in waste.

A KNOCK-OUT PUNCH

But most brilliant and most alarming of all is a new presidential initiative. In July 1997 the news media reported that President Clinton planned to designate ten rivers as "American Heritage Rivers." Special commissars, known as "river navigators," have been created to act as arbiters of what may and may not occur along these waters. Thirteen federal agencies have already become involved with every aspect of life—including zoning controls—on the banks of the designated rivers. Some lawmakers fear that the ten "river communities" are only the beginning of a wholesale federal takeover of the nation's waterways and surroundings.

The concept is as brilliant as it is ominous. Land is useless without water. Why go after land, when the comparatively small number of waterways offers much more efficient means of accomplishing the

same goal? Once again, communism's policy of outright confiscation has been replaced by measures that will yield all the control and
none of the obligations of ownership. Given that incorporating the
Mississippi and its watershed permits control of 40 percent of the
land in the United States with a single stroke of the pen, why spend
time, money, and energy taking on individual property owners?

The process of transforming this country into one that lives by
Franco-Germanic, as opposed to Anglo-American, political tenets is
a lengthy one, because America possesses vast resources. The plenty
with which we are surrounded tends to lull us into a state of lassitude,
and provides an ideal cover for the efforts aimed at curtailing our
freedom. Our material wealth appears to be increasing every day as
Americans once again demonstrate their unlimited capacity to adapt
and adjust. But let us not forget that human potential—and our freedom to develop it fully—is what provides America's real strength.

Maintaining that strength demands that we retain our common
American identity. No one knows that better than those who labor
to extinguish it altogether.

IDENTITY

CHAPTER NINETEEN

ON NATIONAL IDENTITIES

FUNCTIONS OF IDENTITY

"Where are you from?"—the frequency with which this question is asked reveals an endless fascination with identity. Cheering erupts when the name of a state or a town is mentioned by a talk show host, featured speaker, or stand-up comedian, if anyone present comes from that locality.

Identity is an unalienable part of being. These days, children in our schools are encouraged early on to think of themselves in terms of racial and sexual identity. Increasingly, people describe themselves by the ethnic identity of their ancestors. Why is every kind of identity encouraged, yet our sense of national identity scorned?

Perhaps the entire concept of national identity has fallen into disfavor. But wait. When it comes to merchandise, we seem to be quite particular. I just bought some dried "organic Turkish apricots, Swiss certified." That is national identity twice over.

Yet focusing on *people's* national identity is deemed "reactionary"—a harmful throwback to times and places from which we wish to distance ourselves. National identity, we are told, became an instrument of exclusion, a tool to emphasize differences between peoples, something we need to avoid and eliminate (there is that word again). Consequently, we are actively discouraged to think of ourselves as "American." What has caused national identity to be viewed as nefarious?

NATIONALISM AND "INTERNATIONALISM"

In a word, the Third Reich. As well as categorizing people according to race, it ranked nationalities according to their respective "worth." The Third Reich employed the concept not only to categorize people, but also to exterminate them by the millions.

Could the desire to put distance between ourselves and the nazis be the sole reason we cannot be Americans? As with the other puzzles addressed on these pages, we need to dig deeper and discover that, yet again, contemporary America has to grapple with crises that occurred in France and Germany long ago and have nothing to do with us.

Source No. 1: *Chauvinism* is a French word, stemming from the name of an actual person whose super-patriotism and attachment to Napoleon, shared by multitudes for decades, suddenly became an object of ridicule in France after 1830. The original sentiment, and subsequent pejorative application of the word, reveal an ongoing split in French attitudes.

Source No. 2: While France and—significantly—England had become nations, Germany, for centuries, remained a conglomerate of kingdoms, principalities, fiefdoms, and bishoprics. Before Otto von Bismarck, in 1871, united the territories and proclaimed a single Germany, German thinkers and writers had concluded that national identity was indispensable to national greatness. During the eighteenth century, they became obsessed with the question of German identity—their agony still reflected in Richard Wagner's 1865 essay, "Was ist Deutsch?" (What does it mean to be German?).

But better known to American readers is Friedrich Schiller's "Ode to Joy," immortalized in Beethoven's Ninth Symphony. In it, the poet who extolled national identity in his plays *Don Carlos* and *William Tell*, commits himself to Internationalism in the line, "All humans shall be brothers"—possibly inspiring Marx's call, "Proletarians of the World: Unite!" So much for the split in German attitudes.

Eventually, two ideas of French revolutionary origin—egalitarianism and internationalism—emerged on top. Egalitarianism became the "ideal" arrangement within a given society, and internationalism the preferred arrangement for the coexistence of different societies. Both, as we know, were adopted by the Russian revolution of 1917.

Several incarnations of "The International" ("a federation of working-class parties aiming at the transformation of the capitalist societies into socialist commonwealths"), and its successor, the "Communist International," were organized on the premise that only the working classes were qualified to create, and rule over, a world united in the name of social justice. After the Second World War the organization was reconvened in Frankfurt, Germany, under the name "Socialist International."

The concept of internationalism prescribes that countries and their residents look upon all other countries and *their* residents as brothers, equals, and partners in various endeavors. Once achieved, such a state of mind is expected to do away with wars, just as communism—perfect social justice—is supposed to erase economic, intellectual, racial, class, or other tensions within a given society. Internationalism, then, is by definition a part of the Franco-Germanic political agenda and useful to communists as a slogan.

In reality, both Germany and Russia were nationalists at heart. The only difference was that Russia, especially in its Soviet phase, added a large dose of internationalist hypocrisy to the rhetoric. The practice was to settle large numbers of Russians in the "other republics" of the Inner Empire (Ukraine, Georgia, Lithuania, and so forth). In the Outer Empire—Poland, Bulgaria, Hungary, Czechoslovakia—the armies wore Russian uniforms, the state emblems were variations of the Soviet model, "Heroes of the Soviet Union" were worshiped, and soccer players had to avoid scoring when playing Soviet teams. As with every other aspect of the Ideology, "internationalism" is a euphemism—in this instance, the substitution of a supra-national authority for previously autonomous nation-states.

"Internationalism" is also useful in separating "good people" from "evil people." Nationalism is "evil," and internationalism is "good." Illustrations of "evil" used to rely exclusively on shades of the Third Reich. Of late, the breakup of Yugoslavia and the atrocities in Bosnia have been added to the "evil nationalism" side (ignoring the fact that Yugoslavia was not a "nation" to begin with). The United Nations with its "humanitarian" agencies, and the European Union, are automatically "good" since they embody the international concept.

NATIONALISM AND HYPOCRISY

Currently fashionable doctrines brand any awareness of one's nationality as "nationalism" because it is supposed to drive a wedge between peoples and, sooner or later, result in war.

But there is a world of difference between nationalism and a healthy sense of national identity. In the first place, national identity is neither an "-ism" nor a wedge. Rather, it is a magnet. It is also an umbrella under which the assets, sentiments, and goals of the largest number of compatible people may be combined. Furthermore, war is not a function of national identity. If disputes about possessions, or simple hostility between two groups, reach a certain stage, war will break out whether the ground is religious, tribal, or economic. To blame a sense of national identity for war is either ignorance of history, or hypocrisy.

There is much hypocrisy in the actions of those who advocate the Franco-Germanic political philosophy. The second half of the twentieth century continued the creation of "nations," begun at the end of

World War I, but on a scale unimaginable just a short while ago. The deluge started with the decolonization of Africa, where tribes clearly unable to coexist have been forced into national entities. It continued with the breakup of the Russian empire. (I use "Russian," because most of the empire had been annexed well before the Soviet phase.) Millions have lived for centuries as tribes, or ethnic regions, with little or no concept of a national existence. But since membership in the United Nations is predicated on being a "nation," some form of "nationalism" needed to be fostered in those lands.

This reasoning has led to the emergence of new "nations" in Europe and Asia, and fuels nation-building efforts in Haiti and Bosnia. In order to function and succeed as a nation, however, certain prerequisites are necessary. Among these are natural resources capable of sustaining the population either directly or through trade, and the ability to build cities, to organize production and distribution, to establish and maintain communications, to operate an educational system—in short, the ability to stand on one's own two feet. The spectacle of creating "nation" after "nation" in places where not even a fraction of these prerequisites exists is proof of a new reality: existence outside the nation-state has become practically impossible. Assistance from the World Bank and the International Monetary Fund is available only to nations, as is participation in international events. The opening ceremonies of the 1996 Olympic Games featured 197 "nations," some of which were stretched to the limit by the requirement to produce national uniforms and fly a delegation to Atlanta.

Encouraging all these "nations" to emerge, while disparaging "nationalism," is the height of hypocrisy—so is blaming nationalism for tensions and failures that exist precisely because nation-states were encouraged where none had existed. And what of the support expressed for every separatist movement—be it Quebec in Canada or Wales in Great Britain—by those who complain loudest about "nationalism"?

The fact is that national identity is an instrument of internal cohesion and induces people to *disregard* their differences, including differences of class. Marx's view of history, as we have seen, was: "The history of all hitherto existing society is the history of class struggle." Were national identity recognized as an aspiration of the people, Marx's view could not be sustained. Worse still, any acknowledgment that national identity mitigates class differences and unites people within a society would cause Marx's entire theory of history—and with it entire departments of history at American universities—to collapse.

CHAPTER TWENTY

AMERICAN IDENTITY

A CONDITION OF LIBERTY

National identity is an excellent lens through which to examine differences between the Franco-Germanic and Anglo-American ways of thinking. The former, if you will recall, develops the theory and expects events to conform. The latter observes events, endeavors to draw conclusions from them, and formulates policies based on the lessons learned.

Accordingly, Franco-Germanic theorists have written extensively, and are writing again, about the nature of national identity, and whether it really exists. On the Anglo-American side, the empirical evidence is sufficient to conclude that the attainment and retention of liberty has occurred in tandem with national identity. While national identity, in and of itself, does not guarantee freedom, freedom in sophisticated societies has not been known to exist, and defense of freedom would not be feasible, without a concurrent sense of national identity. (Next to England and America, the birth of the Netherlands around 1600 and the attendant immediate prosperity serves as the best example.) But the inverse also holds true: We seem to be losing our liberties—freedom of speech, freedom of association—in direct proportion to our loss of American identity.

Compared with other nations, America's identity had to be constructed of uncommon ingredients. It was. America's identity was called upon to function differently from the rest. It did. America's identity had to be unique if the United States were to succeed as a nation. It is.

Ordinarily, ingredients of national identity are comprised of a common ethnic origin; a shared history; a language, traditions, and culture developed together over time; and a religion common to all or most inhabitants. National identity *emerge*s as a compendium of some or all of these.

This applies to countries that evolve gradually, recasting the structure of society as circumstances change. Those countries, those nations, have always been—and are likely to remain—"works in progress."

UNIQUE CIRCUMSTANCES

By contrast, the United States of America came into being through a single act of creation, even if completion of the act took several years. The ingredients ordinarily available to other nations were clearly unavailable to the Founders. Yet, the need for a national identity was compelling here as nowhere else. "The name of AMERICAN," said George Washington in his farewell address, "which belongs to you, in your national capacity, must always exalt the just pride of Patriotism, more than any appellation derived from local discriminations." Later, Washington spoke of a "national morality," something that could not exist except as an ingredient of a national character. And, by the time Alexis de Tocqueville came to chronicle the ways of America, a national character—identity, really—was there for all to observe.

Again: a nation with no history as a nation, coming into existence by design as opposed to evolution, has to rely on uncommon ingredients to secure its identity. Nowhere else would present and future differences in ethnicity, language, custom, culture, and religion be so *difficult* to reconcile. Nowhere else would present and future differences in ethnicity, language, custom, culture, and religion be so *crucial* to reconcile. Indeed, if ever national identity needed to serve as a magnet, it was in America. Theodore Roosevelt said that "The one absolutely certain way of bringing this nation to ruin, of preventing all possibility of its continuing to be a nation at all, would be to permit it to become a tangle of squabbling nationalities."

The ingredients came about by *agreement*. In place of a shared history, a shared belief in and adherence to certain legal and political principles—overwhelmingly of British origin—were substituted. A common language would facilitate the development of a common culture over time. To ensure freedom of conscience and an atmosphere of tolerance, no state religion would be established, but a Bible-based morality was taken for granted. Additional characteristics included a strong work ethic, an expectation of competence, a spirit of voluntary cooperation, an insistence on free choice, and a fierce sense of independence. Together, they created a national talent for entrepreneurship. Then, to compensate for the absence of common ethnic roots, the appellation *American* was made available to original colonist and naturalized immigrant alike. Indeed, the offer of that appellation became the strongest magnet for newcomers. Elsewhere, immigrants might become subjects, even citizens. But a person not born there could never become English, or French, or German. Every immigrant admitted to this country is welcome to become *American*.

PRINCIPLES AND LANGUAGE

Considering the ingredients of American identity one by one, we find our legal and political principles articulated in the founding documents—the Declaration of Independence, the Constitution of the United States, and the Federalist Papers. We might look upon them as the equivalent of what the corporate world calls "Articles of Incorporation" and "Bylaws." The deal offered to every man, woman, and child was, and is, a simple one: Obtain a permit, get yourself over, and sign on to our principles as published in our "Articles and Bylaws." Once you sign on and adhere to them, we will share with you the liberties, the opportunities, and the riches of our land.

For language, America chose to stay with English—not merely because the founders spoke it. Languages have much to do with the traditions, with the institutions they transmit. Language helps define the institutions, and these in turn influence the language as it continues to evolve. Children, as they grow up, are affected by the language they hear and learn to speak. Processes are affected by the language that governs them. Language, then, reflects existing attitudes in a society, as much as it determines future ones. Given what we know about the origins and nature of our institutions, it seems obvious that their development was profoundly affected by, and their continued existence largely predicated upon, the English language. And, while knowledge of other languages opens great vistas in literature, commerce, and travel, the legal and political institutions which are transmitted through other languages were examined and rejected at the time of America's founding, and since.

MORALITY AND ETHICS

Perhaps because there is no coercive state religion, Americans, for the most part, have always remained deeply religious. The search for freedom of conscience brought, and brings, many a newcomer to these shores. Consequently, far more denominations exist in America than anywhere else and, for the most part, they are Christian. For two centuries, no one questioned the obvious. It was understood that, while everyone was free to believe and practice as conscience dictated, the moral foundations of America rested on the Old and New Testaments of the Bible. The founders enacted few laws partly because they understood the wisdom that the fewer the laws, the broader the agreement. At the same time, they saw no *need* for certain secular laws, because of what they regarded as God's law. In their thinking, the Bible was a given. The combination of all these factors rendered American society infinitely more tolerant than any other.

While it is easy for critics to point out instances in which greater tolerance might have been displayed, those same critics would find it difficult to cite an example of similar, much less greater, religious tolerance elsewhere. We know that the persecution of Jews was characteristic of both the Third Reich and the Soviet Union. The ongoing persecution of Christians both in the Muslim and Buddhist world has been frequently documented. What used to be India had to be split along religious lines. And in Bosnia, people of different religions are poised to resume killing one another as soon as the last foreign soldier departs.

The work ethic, and competence in one's chosen endeavor, not only allowed Americans to achieve affluence and create abundance, they were also great equalizers. The idea that everyone ought to work was a powerful mitigator of the different circumstances of birth. Of even greater consequence was the respect for competence which, in American society, replaced the scale of values assigned to various types of work. It was not *what* one did, but *how* one did it that mattered. Competence was expected whether a person swept floors or split atoms.

The apparently separate concepts of voluntary cooperation, freedom of choice, and fierce independence are in reality closely interwoven. The sense of independence ensured that cooperation would be sought only if circumstances warranted, in which case benefits would accrue to all participants. The freedom of choice enabled everyone to weigh expected benefits against potential disadvantage, and to decide accordingly. Nowhere do we observe these ingredients of American identity more successfully at work than in cases of need. In 1834, a year before Alexis de Tocqueville wrote *Democracy in America*, an author from Transylvania (then Hungary) Sándor Bölöni Farkas, published a book about his North American travels in which he marveled at the astonishing capacity of communities in the United States to look after the less fortunate in their midst. He ascribed that, as well as countless other "miracles" he had observed, to a degree of freedom not to be found on the continent of Europe.

These, then, were the ingredients of American identity. Together, they created a society in which those who swept floors today could dream of splitting the atom tomorrow.

UNDER FIRE

Many today are engaged in replacing these ingredients. Substitutions are advocated and practiced in literally every area that affects American identity. Customarily, the opening salvo of the battle is to postulate that an American identity does not exist. Our strength, the suggestion goes, is in our "diversity."

As the case with "social justice" and all its derivatives, no explanation—much less a definition—exists of the word "diversity." All we are told is that diversity is "good."

Since diversity has been a characteristic of the United States from the very beginning—most Americans can point to a healthy mixture of ancestors—just any kind of diversity obviously won't do. It must then be a certain and specific kind of diversity. And, as we know, strict quotas established by advocates of "social justice" regulate diversity. That, in turn, means that persons whose addition or inclusion makes the mix "correct" are of a specific and recognizable identity. A look at any local television newscast will demonstrate the required composition which is, in fact, anything but diverse. The customary cast of four (two for news, one each for sports and weather) must contain one woman, one black person (any gender), and, if available, one Hispanic.

Thus, far from eliminating the sense of identity in general, it is only the *American* identity that must be obliterated by other identities. And nothing will more certainly obliterate that which is the sum of ingredients than the substitution of different ingredients. Indeed, we have already seen the substitution of the search for social justice for the rule of law, the substitution of group rights for individual rights, and the substitution of entitlements for the guarantee of property. If we now take stock of the ingredients of American identity, the scenario is no less alarming.

The long-standing expectation that those wishing to live among us learn, comprehend, and embrace the legal and political principles that form the foundations of our society has been all but abandoned. Our common language is under attack everywhere, the attack camouflaged as "accommodation" for those who come here, and for their children. In what is perhaps the strangest twist of all, religious people have been classified by most media commentators and liberal politicians as "evil" because they would rob the "good" people of their freedom by advocating moral values. George Washington's "national morality" has been erased by jettisoning restraint in all areas of human conduct. Closely connected to this is the abandonment of *effort* as a prerequisite of reward, the corresponding loss of the work ethic, and any need for competence. None is compatible with the process known as affirmative action. It follows that voluntary cooperation is no longer possible, for the prerequisite of that is voluntary association. The arrival of a "voluntarism project" run by commissars was only a matter of time, since commissars had already claimed the prerogative to determine who does not need to work, who is rewarded, and who is going to be declared "competent."

"CHANGE" UNMASKED

Thus, every ingredient of American identity is in the process of being permanently replaced—some to atone for past "ills," some simply for the sake of "change." Change has become a "good" word. Change is good because "nothing should go on forever." But would any of us trade a car that always starts, for one that spends three-quarters of its time in the workshop? Would any of us knowingly give up advanced plumbing for a hole in the ground? Change, then, is not good in and of itself. Yet we are abandoning our recipe for a successful society because we have been persuaded that all proposed changes will be for the better—that the changes will enhance, without materially to alter, the ability of this society to succeed.

And here we find our old friend, "CBS"—Compartmentalized Brain Syndrome—which impedes the transference of knowledge from one compartment of our brain to another. Although our society is unique in the history of the world, we seem suddenly to have forgotten the ingredients that make up the recipe. Worse still, we haven't forgotten—we simply ignore them.

What has happened to our common sense that could make us believe we can change all the ingredients, and still retain the original article? How can we honestly believe that, say, ground beef, mustard, and Worcestershire sauce will combine into chocolate ice cream?

And, if we understand that different ingredients will result in a society altogether different from the one established here some two hundred years ago, why are we willing to countenance the "change" without so much as an honest, open debate?

CHAPTER TWENTY-ONE

THE WORLD OF AFFIRMATIVE ACTION

NOT WHAT YOU THINK

The title of this chapter does not refer to a program adopted in the United States during the 1970s as a temporary means by which to accelerate the integration of black Americans. Rather, it points to an attitude, adopted globally, which has pervaded every aspect of our lives, and which has distorted every area of our endeavors. In this sense, affirmative action represents a determination to compensate for the shortcomings of God, Nature, History, and Happenstance.

The result is a continuous redistribution and reallocation of human accomplishment, of results and rewards, of events that occurred in the past, and of future opportunities. The identical approach operates in scenarios as diverse as the finals of World Cup Soccer, the risking of the life of an American astronaut as he floats inside dysfunctional metal tubes the Russians call "Space Station Mir," or a manual sporting the lofty title: *National Standards for United States History*. In all its countless forms, affirmative action is only one more manifestation of "the search for social justice," of Franco-Germanic political philosophy, of the road toward communism.

CREATING AND RESTORING "BALANCE"

Soccer, the dominant spectator sport of Europe and Latin America, has long celebrated a tournament of its best by assembling the top sixteen teams of the world every four years. The coveted places in the finals used to go to winners of a round robin competition. No more. Affirmative action has been applied to make certain that all the peoples of the world are represented in the finals. As a result, several European and Latin American teams, which would normally have qualified, sit at home while Asian, African, and North American teams, years away from World Cup standards, take their place. Apparently, it was judged "unfair" to exclude entire continents, just because their teams were not good enough. The last two soccer World Cups elicited a worldwide yawn.

"Fairness to Russia" is a recurring theme. Ethel and Julius Rosenberg, and others around them, judged it "unfair" for the United States to possess nuclear technology, while Russia did not. In the movie Failsafe, the American president offers to destroy New York City to "balance" the effects of an accidently launched missile. Currently, the money of American taxpayers, the know-how and the lives of Americans may be sacrificed to make up for Russia's failures in space. Princely sums are transferred, technology shared, and lives risked in the name of "joint" space exploration with a country that has yet to figure out a way to organize the production and distribution of bread.

HISTORY STANDARDS

But the worst is the project known as *National Standards for United States History*. It has been used to misrepresent the past and to create an entire web of fiction that will be difficult, if not impossible, to disentangle. The publication was best described in an editorial in the *New York Times*: "And Now a History for the Rest of Us." Indeed. As well as socking it to everyone and everything the authors dislike—basically the English-speaking world—*National Standards for United States History* hands "a place in history" to vast numbers of people who never made it into the real thing. For the most part, it is a collection of names and events either fabricated, or simply irrelevant to history courses in grade school or high school. Most students, knowing little history, need basic facts, names, and a time grid for orientation. The authors of the *Standards* have no such purpose in mind.

The approach is revealed in the title of the opening chapter: "Three Worlds Meet." The creation of the United States is predicated on the "great convergence of West African, Native American, and West-European peoples." A sane mind cannot contemplate the United States of America and fail to observe that its way of life grew distinctly from the last of the three proposed "worlds." Predictably, this chapter pays a great deal of attention to African, and what is now called "Native" American, antecedents, with only a perfunctory nod to Europe. The "three worlds," moreover, appear to be in comparable stages of development. To put it graphically, the starting assumption is the equivalence of a grass hut, or a teepee, with London, Paris, Rome, Madrid, Florence, Vienna... the list is endless.

Why do the leading historians of America engage in writing utter nonsense? All plausible answers lead to the proposition on these pages.

The first order of business seems to have been a desire to *redistribute credit* for accomplishment. The authors clearly felt that Europe—western civilization—has been credited for so much, and for so long, that it must be "unfair" by definition. The time has come to spread it around. Advocates call it "restoring balance," the implication being that they are merely correcting an anomaly. According to such views, previously accepted histories exaggerated the importance of the European side at the expense of the others. The United States, *Standards* asserts, is the result of the cross-fertilization and fusion of ideas and practices that evolved in West Africa, among various North American Indian tribes, and, also, in Europe.

Such assertions, of course, suffer from a paucity of evidence. Among the three lineages listed, writing histories was characteristic of only one, Europe, which alone possessed the means—the art of writing. *Standards* resolves this quandary by *constructing histories* for the non-European participants as the second order of business. One way of doing this is to invent and attach unrealistic significance to certain events and practices. Examples range from tales about the "great wealth and grandeur" of the court of Mansa Musa, a fourteenth-century ruler in Mali, to the Iroquois origins of the U.S. Constitution. Attention is directed to the "Myths and Legends of the Haida Indians of the Northwest," and to "Mississippian, Aztec, Mayan, Incan, Iroquois, Pueblo, and Inuit societies," as well as to "Hopi and Zuni cultures of the Southwest." To gain insight into Africa, "Muslim scholars such as Ibn Fadi Allah al-Omari and Ibn Battuta" are to be read, and "major urban centers such as Timbuktu and Jenne" studied. There is not even a perfunctory attempt to depict contemporaneous Europe and its incomparable sophistication in every field.

An additional tool of significance was to place emphasis on, and give enormous space to, discussions of the oppressed and the exploited. A corresponding suppression of events and personalities critical in the making and building of America is seen—or rather not seen—in the pictorial illustrations. Affirmative action at work. The predominance of white males among America's founders, leaders, explorers, inventors, and industrial pioneers must have impressed the authors also as "unfair." The way to restore balance was to ignore them altogether.

Another ploy is the manipulation of blame, as in the case of the Cold War. The authors ignore that, following World War II, the United States dismantled its military apparatus, while the Soviets did nothing of the sort. They ignore that the United States turned Germany (West) and Japan into peaceful, democratic states, while the Soviets established a reign of terror over the Eastern half of

Europe, took Berlin under blockade, and encouraged North Korea to attack South Korea. Predictably, restraint of the American response—demonstrated by the famous airlift to supply Berlin, and by restoring *status quo* in Korea—is ignored as well.

The most carefully calculated damage, however, is inflicted by recurring references to America's "peoples," thereby denying the existence of an American identity. Indian tribes are often characterized as "nations," but the United States never is. Our country is portrayed as an ongoing struggle between the oppressed, who are obviously "good," and the forces of "evil," represented by white males, individually and collectively.

AN "-ISM" FOR WOMEN ONLY

In *Standards*, women are in irreconcilable opposition to men, excepting, one supposes, oppressed blacks and Hispanics—and the authors of *Standards*. Women, of course, have come to play a crucial role in the "World of Affirmative Action." Some even fear that women, having weighed the advantages, will want to hang on long after black Americans call it a day.

The basic thesis of feminism is that women have been oppressed by men since time immemorial. As with other "-isms," feminism derives from Franco-Germanic thought, in that it predicates a political posture upon an innate condition, and pits two groups against one another in irreconcilable hostility from which no member of the group may be exempt. Feminist sentiments range from resentment at the exclusion of women from certain occupations to maintaining that every form of sexual contact is rape. Those of the latter persuasion hold that children ought to be conceived through artificial insemination, and preferably brought up by a lesbian couple.

As in many other instances, ignorance of history is an important prerequisite for the maintenance of affirmative action attitudes; in the present case, ignoring nature is another. As opposed to earlier, legitimate demands for participation and equitable compensation, feminism in the 1990s is the myopia of women sitting in climate-controlled offices. Relieved of the chores and duties of the ages by a battery of machines, they make pronouncements ignoring the thousands of years directly preceding our century during which survival of the species had to be the primary consideration.

No one can deny that, in the course of history, women often found themselves in a subordinate position—though by no means always or in every society. But at the same time, women were protected, and in many an epoch placed on a pedestal. In any event, the complex and varied role of women through the ages cannot be reduced to a simplistic slogan describing one half of all human beings as "the victims of history." Those who say so have a quarrel with God, or with nature, or simply with facts.

RESPONSIBILITY AND THE CRISIS OF IDENTITY

Restraints, remember, must be accepted as a prerequisite of *rights*. Just as rights and restraints form a pair that ought not to be severed, our participation in society does not amount to prerogatives only; it also requires the acceptance of *responsibilities or obligations*. Men have traditionally, indeed automatically, accepted the responsibilities and obligations that attend their place in society. In the euphoria of women doing "everything men can do, and more, and better," a discussion of their corresponding obligations has yet to surface. The responsibility for maintaining the home has been thrown overboard like so much excess baggage. At the same time, women's very identity is in crisis. Increasingly, on screens big and small, we encounter women spouting obscenities or kicking men in the groin, while other women applaud hysterically.

The obligation to bear children and be the center of family life was not imposed on women by the cruelty of men. These are vital constituents of our existence. Passing on custom, manners, and knowledge to the young, preparing food, keeping house, are all indispensable functions. If women found it unrewarding, the answer is that men, too, have had to engage in many an unrewarding activity. If women found themselves insufficiently appreciated, the remedy is to demand appreciation in word and deed. If women found it too difficult, it should be remembered that men have endeavored to alleviate as much of it as possible. The desire to make a woman's life easier has been, in fact, a main engine of America's affluence.

And here, the unprecedented affluence of American society meets the World of Affirmative Action. Today, it is possible to be employed in a specific occupation, not because society needs it, but because a person *wants* it, or because "social justice" demands it. Society has no more need for "a black woman to teach law at Harvard" than it has, at this stage, for a "teacher in orbit," unless, that is, a brilliant jurist happens to be a black woman, or a teacher qualifies as an astronaut. But this is not the case in the World of Affirmative Action, which calls for the participation in certain endeavors by certain people because of the pigment in their skin, their genital configuration, or both.

Great thinkers, statesmen, scientists, artists, explorers, and inventors—alas, predominantly white males to date—have always labored for everyone's benefit. So have all others who have *earned* a genuine place in history, such as Jane Austen, Madame Curie, or Nat King Cole. Today, those who are clamoring for recognition will have to rise above their current exclusive preoccupation with "their own thing." As long as a woman shows concern only for women, as long as a black person shows interest only in black issues, they will remain confined to the World of Affirmative Action.

And that world is ruled by commissars. It cannot exist in a society of free citizens.

CHAPTER TWENTY-TWO

BRIDGEHEADS

REGARDING HOLLYWOOD

Complaints about the "demeaning ways" in which women were represented before the advent of affirmative action fly in the face of evidence exemplified by movies produced during those decades when Hollywood was primarily a reflection of American society, as opposed to the bully pulpit it has become. Women of granite character were portrayed by the likes of Bette Davis, Katherine Hepburn, and Greer Garson. These women knew how to assert their strength without kicks in the groin, and their wisdom without acrimony. Their strength and wisdom were combined with grace and wit. And who could miss the towering contributions of the women who built and maintained the homesteads in the West?

But those were the decades when the cinema was an art form, and America's own art form at that. It could create characters to represent both what we are and what we would wish to be. It communicated fear and despair without hysteria. It filled us with the terror of war without blood and gore. It showed us love and passion without the sound and fury.

In the many tales of "right and wrong," the underlying message

was that Americans were expected to conduct themselves in ways
that were "right." Imbedded in the message was another one,
namely, that America was a place where "right" prevailed. In *Mr.
Smith Goes to Washington*, the adversary Jimmy Stewart takes on is
not America, but a senator who flaunts America's code of conduct.
In *Twelve Angry Men*, Henry Fonda demonstrates that, even when
eleven out of twelve jurors fall prey to inertia and group psychology,
the system works. Individuals were cast as "bad guys," but always for
something they had done, not because of the "group" they represented. And when time came for advocacy, Hollywood knew how to
present it as art.

But all that has changed. By the end of the 1960s, Hollywood
began to take on the role of a bridgehead for the forces of Franco-
Germanic thought, a bridgehead in the search for social justice. In
this new scenario, America was no longer "right." Worse yet,
instead of "right and wrong" being what individual persons *did*, the
message became that "good and evil" was in what people, represent-
ing specific groups, *were*.

Early notice was served in *The Candidate*. The 1972 film, starring
Robert Redford, casts the incumbent senator whom Redford challenges (a Republican, naturally) as a shallow, pompous, empty-
headed operator. It is through the lips of such a character that we
hear a reaffirmation of America's founding principles. "I tell you
this," the incumbent proclaims at a cookout, "that I still believe individuals are responsible for themselves." And later: "My friends, the
issue is whether we are going to hold on to the most successful philosophy in the history of mankind, or whether we are going to trade
it in for a collectivist state. This philosophy is the work of free individuals. Free enterprise has made this nation great...." These lines
are delivered as a caricature of what might have sat quite naturally
on the tongue of a Jimmy Stewart. But Redford, his 1972 counterpart, marched to a different beat. "This is a society," Redford's character explodes at the end of his televised debate, "divided by fear,

hatred, and violence. Until we talk about just what this society really is, I don't know how we are going to change it!" And off he charges to eventual victory.

"GOOD" AND "EVIL" GROUPS

But in 1972 there was still room for a bit of humor, for a moment of relief amidst the incessant lectures the film dispenses about the environment, healthcare, race, poverty, inadequate housing, and unemployment. As he is driven to his umpteenth rally of the day, Redford (as Bill McKay, the candidate) is musing in the backseat of his limo. "I say to you, can't any longer—Oh-h no—can't any longer—play off black against old, young against poor. This country cannot house its houseless, feed its foodless, a-a-and on election day—a-a-and on election day!—vote once, vote tw-wice, for Bill McKay!"

There is no longer room for mixing the political agenda with humor in *Regarding Henry* (1991, Harrison Ford), the story of a white New York attorney who is the embodiment of evil. His lucrative career is built on winning for the bad guys. In the office, he treats his obviously terrified elderly lady secretary like a dog. In private life, he cheats on his beautiful and unhappy wife, and castigates his permanently sour-faced little girl, Rachel, about responsibility. One evening, as he is buying cigarettes (he is a smoker, naturally), Henry is shot in the head by a punk. Although he recovers physically, he is unable to speak, walk, or recognize his family. And here, the real story begins.

After a series of inane and useless attempts by white physicians, therapists, and his own family to elicit a response, Henry is turned over to the care of Bradley, a black male physical therapist. Bradley teaches Henry to walk again, and takes it upon himself to shock Henry into speaking. Under his care, Henry makes rapid progress. Henry has to learn everything from scratch, but he is now obviously a "good" person: The morning after he throws all his pillows (a ridiculous luxury!) out of the bed, he competes with his daughter in knocking over glasses full of fruit juice at the breakfast table. Father and daughter are reconciled in this symbolic embrace and Rachel, now at ease, teaches her father to read again. She also reminds Henry of family stories of old. "Your father," Rachel recites with obvious resentment, "used to make you mow the lawn, *and* take out the garbage, *and* walk the dog, *and* wash the car, and then 'you'll learn to appreciate the work ethic.'" "What's that?" Henry asks, dumbfounded. "I don't know," replies Rachel, now sporting the smile of angels.

The rest is a foregone conclusion. Henry walks out of his law firm, helps the last victim of his "evil" existence to retry the previously lost case, forsakes the rows of suits hanging in his closets, declares his distaste for steak and eggs, and moves to the country. His last act is to burst into the assembly hall of the academy Rachel attends and remove his daughter as the principal holds forth on the subject of work ethic. The verdict on Henry is delivered by Rosella, the Hispanic maid: "I going to miss you, Mister Henry. I like you much better now!" The source of "good" is Bradley; the source of authoritative approval is Rosella.

Just five years later, we find the "good" scenario fully developed in *My Fellow Americans*. Two former presidents, played by Jack Lemmon (Republican) and James Garner (Democrat), find themselves on the run from a band of national security agents. They are to be killed on orders from the National Security Agency in an effort to hush up a kickback scandal brewing around the incumbent president. The storyline is relevant only to the extent that it portrays every white male as corrupt, demented, or an imbecile. The two "heroes" serve mostly as props to ridicule the presidency—advantage given to the Democrat, of course. As they scramble to stay alive and get to some documents that would confirm their clear record, the fugitives encounter a wide range of people whose help they need—the "good" people. The black "quota" is perfectly balanced: An elderly male owner of a diner is the only one to offer food without payment; the female cook in the White House provides cover and motherly care; exchanges with a young Secret Service agent drive home the point that the Republican president does not even notice his existence. Hispanics are represented through an illegal immigrant from Mexico, trying for the fourth time to slip into his "beloved home, America," who insists on giving his only possession—a compass!—to the Democrat who had lent him his overcoat.

Next, we are in the middle of a Gay Activist parade. One of the men dressed as "Dorothy" in *The Wizard of Oz* offers the presidents transportation for the rest of the way. The transportation turns out to be a flock of Dykes on Bikes, causing the Republican to suggest that women ought to be in the military after all. Near the end, our heroes' lives are saved by a sharpshooter stationed with other special units on the roof of the White House. When he is presented to the former presidents, there is a moment of confusion: might it be that a white man in uniform is the instrument of justice after all? It depends on one's definition of man. The sharpshooter winks and lets Lemmon and Garner know that he was "Dorothy" in the gay parade.

Oh, yes. The presidents do meet a white Republican family. The father, who sings America's praise, gets everything wrong and turns out to know nothing about "his beloved country." The child spews waste product through every orifice. The mother is the only person in the film who actually leaves the presidents stranded on the road.

THE HALLS OF ACADEME

As, by Franco-Germanic definition, the "good" groups and "evil" groups took over the screen, knowledge in the classroom was supplanted by programs of similar origin. Because of its predominantly German orientation, academia was primed to be a bridgehead for some time. The special opportunity of the 1960s merely clinched the deal. Selected as primary points of incursion were the Schools of Education, as well as the Schools of Journalism and Departments of

Communication. Schools of Education have always been the weakest link in the academic chain and, at the same time, have assured advocates of the Ideology access to coming generations of students in all age groups. The significance of the other two is obvious, and success in all three areas has been phenomenal. Students majoring in these departments tend to arrive with modest knowledge to begin with, and they are easily persuaded by whatever the faculty chooses to impart. Building layer upon layer, generation upon generation, ideological control of just these few areas of study has provided the commissar establishment with an overwhelming grip on the schoolhouse, the newspapers, and all other media.

As the logical next move, history, political science, language, and literature faculties were enlisted to make favorable decisions about hiring, promotion, and tenure contingent on adherence to the Franco-Germanic line. Environmental and social studies fanned out into outlandish areas of "inquiry," and entire departments were invented to foster group consciousness and group hostility. Suggestions that Women's Studies, African-American Studies, or Hispanic Studies had no legitimate place in the university were met with a barrage of "brandings." Batteries of pseudo-academics have been hard at work to manufacture a body of knowledge to justify these departments, but the myth can be sustained only so long as the commissars rule.

It is most disturbing that all such criticism has been treated much the same as criticism of the party was treated in countries where bolsheviks or nazis were in power. While, in America, no critic has been deported or interned, criticism is now classified as "hate speech"— the first step toward the establishment of "political crime." The result: criticism has been effectively stifled. Martin Heidegger and his fellow national-socialists-turned-communists would be well satisfied: Academic freedom has been all but driven out of the American university.

RELATIVIZATION

But before new concepts of "good" and "evil" could be introduced, *value systems had to be destroyed*. The arts were particularly useful in this because, to some extent, the value of a work of art, the place in history of an artist, remain open to subjective interpretation.

Theodor Adorno's *On the Fetish-Character in Music and the Regression of Listening* is an excellent example of the ease with which art can be used as a tool of political agitation. The essay's 13,000 words, written by a sage of the Frankfurt School, say precious little about music, but much about the "damage inflicted upon it by Capitalism." It sets forth unadulterated Franco-Germanic theory with intermittent musical name-dropping, preached from an Olympian height. The text betrays a modest level of professional qualifications, yet it is judgmental to the extreme.

From such antecedents, the most unqualified persons make definitive pronouncements on the subject of the arts on today's college campuses. For the most part, their assembly-line sentences conjure up—at least for someone of my background—the specter of Communist or National Socialist Party operatives whose education consisted of six-week courses at party schools. Even more disturbing, however, is the state of affairs within the arts community. Decades of pursuing an agenda called *relativization* has wiped away the aesthetic criteria which had taken centuries to refine, and eliminated the process of cultivating one's own taste. According to this new doctrine, neither artist nor artwork carries an inherent value. A Beethoven symphony is the same as the drums from the rain forest, the only difference being in the way we "receive" each of them. Reception, the theory goes, will be determined by the recipient's frame of reference, and as such is both coincidental and variable. Consequently, all music is "sound in space," and everything written is merely a "text." Shakespeare, a semiliterate teenager's notes, or the grocery list—all are texts. Relativization, of course, is yet another version of *Gleichschaltung* (switching to parity), imposed on citizens of the Third Reich. Relativization prepared the ground for the arrival of cultural diversity, also known as "multiculturalism."

"Multiculturalism" has little to do with either "multi" or "culture." It rejects the notion that artists and their creations are the common treasure of all humanity, that the very essence of great art is its ability to cut across the divides of time and geography. In doing so, it denies an individual's opportunity to benefit from the civilizing and unifying effect of art—its primary function—and fosters, predictably, group consciousness. "Multi" is a code word for non-Western categories. "Cultural" is everything from Michelangelo's Sistine Chapel to female genital mutilation in Africa. The "multicultural" vocabulary of branding originates in classic Marxist labels—such as "reactionary" or "progressive"—with its own emotive and mindless additions like "dead white male."

Above all, multiculturalism rejects the existence, or validity, of an *American* identity. In reality, that rejection has been one of its main functions.

THE PLAGUE OF "SECONDARY LITERATURE"

With each successive generation, more and more of those who preach the multicultural gospel are genuinely ignorant of the fact that western civilization is the only culture that is truly diverse. They do not know because, as political agitation replaced aesthetics, so *secondary literature* usurped the place of the original work. Over the last decades, the separation of the student from primary sources has been complete. This laid the ground for the humanities—history, political science, languages, literature, music, and the visual arts—to superimpose the agenda of every political activist on the masterworks of Western Civilization.

As in the case of the *National Standards for United States History*, we watch in frozen disbelief the disinterment and autopsy performed on three thousand years of greatness—not, as it were, by trained pathologists, but by crazed criminal investigators sporting university degrees and tenure. They are looking for "oppression and exploitation," they are groping for rape; they are hoping for signs of "repressed homosexuality." Every passing year, course titles and course contents leave the world of knowledge farther and farther behind. A comparison between university bulletins of 1965 and 1995 shows a tripling of course titles, and the exact inverse in their relevance. A glance at Indiana University's 1995-96 courses in Linguistics turns up three levels in Bambara and Hausa, as well as Haitian Creole, but not a single requirement in a major language. The School of Journalism blatantly offers a course entitled "The Media as Social Institutions." Worst of all, in a growing number of instances there is not even a pretense of teaching, or knowing, what is between the covers of a book—only its "reception" and political utility.

Sadly, arts and humanities were conceded early in the game and have provided the perfect terrain upon which the commissar establishment could consolidate a position of decisive influence. In the exact sciences, nature imposes severe penalties for failure to ascertain facts, and the hope was that the sciences would thus remain planted in solid ground. But from positing that *values* do not exist, it is a relatively small step to asserting that *facts* do not exist either. Chaos theory does to geometry what relativization does to the arts. Declaring mathematics "phallocentric" leads down the same road as *Standards*, now complemented by the removal of America's founding documents from the classroom.

As of now, American universities still draw the most talented students, and continue to produce many a leading scientist. But the foundations are cracked, the edges are frayed, and, unless we change course, it is only a matter of time before the entire edifice collapses. A nation of dysfunctional high school graduates cannot for long resupply its institutions of higher education. Moreover, real science and bogus science cannot coexist for long, and bogus science— "ozone depletion," "global warming"—not only occupies much of the terrain, but enjoys the enthusiastic support of the commissar establishment and, significantly, of the news media.

"...AND THAT'S THE WAY IT IS..."

But not the way it used to be. The previously cited Hungarian publisher Sándor Bölöni Farkas reports thus on the journalistic scene in the America of 1829: "We in Europe think it is magic that elevated every individual of the American people to such high levels of knowledge and cultivation, causing the entire nation to blossom, yet the means are simple and natural. One of these is the publication of newspapers.... Science and knowledge of all kinds are disseminated in so many newspapers, distributed with ease and costing little.... Current statistics show 1,015 such publications in the several states, of which New York State alone has 237—54 of them in New York City."

A hundred and thirty years later, in 1959, the newcomer to America could still find a vibrant scene manned by a press corps dedicated to the responsible discharge of its profession, loyal to America, and committed to the search for truth. But the 1960s ushered in the abdication of responsibility, the disavowal of America, and the dissemination of a specific political agenda as "truth." As we approach the year 2000, most journalists have come to seek stardom and, like film makers, have taken to lecturing the nation. Given that many of them appear to possess inadequate knowledge of the world, the mixture makes for a dangerous situation.

In days gone by, there was a clear separation of news reports from editorial opinion. An editor would determine what to run and what to "kill," but once the report appeared, the reader was left alone to ponder its significance. If the newspaper wished to comment, it would do so on the editorial page. Television, too, followed the tradition by clearly identifying "editorials" after the news had been reported. Television was the first to abandon that practice when it replaced its line-up of distinguished journalists with "personalities." First on television, then increasingly in newspapers, every item carried political approval or disapproval. With the fewest possible exceptions, these reflected the Franco-Germanic way of thinking, the move away from America's founding principles, the preoccupation with "social justice."

WORRISOME ORIGINS, ALARMING EXAMPLES

Once again, an uncomfortable but unavoidable fact: the practice of obligatory political content comes to us from the newspapers of Germany's Third Reich and the Soviet Empire. Schools of Journalism caught the virus in the 1960s. Those who entered the profession with incomplete political preparation were soon converted. Typical was the case of the popular Katie Couric of NBC-TV's *Today*. A friendly and charming new face when she appeared on the scene, sweet Katie was fresh air blowing through the monotony of Bryant Gumbel's politics. But, by the time she was dispatched to confront George Bush in the White House, she had turned into an avenging angel, exuding righteousness and fury.

On one occasion, Katie commiserated with a black pianist, after he had been awarded the prestigious Naumburg prize. "How come no African-American won this before?" Katie asked, accusation rampant in her voice. "Because we live in a racist society" came the standard reply, the mile-long roster of celebrated black musicians notwithstanding. The pianist then sat down and banged out his personal version of a Brahms piece, demonstrating that the music profession—never before accused of racism—had in fact succumbed to affirmative action.

On another occasion Joan Lunden opened "Women's Health Week" on ABC-TV's *Good Morning America* with the admonishment, "It is time that medical science begins to pay attention to women's health. It cannot be just for men anymore." What stage of Compartmentalized Brain Syndrome would cause a person to say such a thing?

THE ALL-PURPOSE LAUGHTER

Nothing demonstrates more clearly the abdication of traditional journalistic responsibility than the invention of the all-encompassing phrase "the public's right to know." Where would such a right originate? The purpose of inventing this right is to provide journalists with an excuse to abdicate their responsibility, which includes decency in the affairs of man, loyalty to one's country, and respect for the national interest. All these have been eliminated—first in the classroom, then in the entertainment and news media. In a world of "good" and "evil" groups, foolproof means need to be developed to ensure that "evil" always loses. Control of news items and infusion of editorial opinion can go only so far. For the time being, it is almost impossible in America not to afford some space to the other side. What to do when those who argue the case for America's founding principles have the floor and—Heaven forbid!—begin to make a powerful case?

Enter laughter. As far back as Plato's *Gorgias*, laughter has been used in dialogue as a means to hide the inadequacy of an argument. In our time, laughter has acquired a pivotal role on television. Every time a serious exposition of principles begins to unfold, the resident agent for social justice breaks into sarcastic laughter. As if programmed, the camera switches instantly to the laughing person and the sound of the laughter drowns out most of the opponent's words. Since discussion of serious ideas does not lend itself to hilarity, being laughed at ruffles speakers and, with every cascade of laughter, they look increasingly pedantic and pitiful. The technique is applied every day, whether by Bill Press and Geraldine Ferraro on CNN's *Crossfire*, or Al Hunt on *Capital Gang*. Politicians on the Franco-Germanic side do likewise, as if all had attended the same "School of Derisory Laughter."

The body politic is already distorted by the suppression of certain stories and by the ceaseless repetition of others, by this key word embedded or that key word omitted. Laughter is the ultimate weapon in an already rich arsenal used to attack America's founding principles. And the faces—ah, the faces! They tell the story a thousand times over. Watch our "TV personalities" interview someone from the "good" side; then someone from the "evil" side. Here, overcome with admiration, the face glows, the voice signals agreement, the questions are apologetic. There, the face is severe, the voice cold and demanding, the questions abrasive.

That is how far we have come.

CHAPTER TWENTY-THREE

COUNTLESS BATTLEFIELDS—
ONE BATTLE

MONEY

Lingering doubts about Franco-Germanic insistence that the world be divided into "good" and "evil" will be dispelled by looking at the current distribution of unearned money. This money tends to come from four sources: government subsidies, foundations, corporate charity, and private donations. According to all available literature, the majority of great foundations—Carnegie, Ford, MacArthur, Rockefeller, Pew—switched their support from the generally worthy to the politically "good" causes even before the government did. Once government signed on, it was only a matter of time before corporations saw the wisdom of marching in step. Private giving is the only area where support is spread across the political spectrum.

Causes classified as "good" include the subsidy of all persons who claim that they or their ancestors suffered some form of unfair treatment. In evaluating grant applications, for example, the applicant's suitability to the task matters no more than the nature of the proposal. It matters even less whether the use of funds is compatible with the purpose designated for the foundation by its original founder. A similar attitude governs decisions about scholarly projects. So long as the proposal contains something new, preferably in opposition to everything that has gone before, no questions are asked about its worth or rationality. A glance at the list of recipients of MacArthur's annual "genius awards," or at papers given at annual conventions of the Modern Languages Association will attest to the preferred topics. The latter includes panels on "Chicano Literature," "Gendering British Aestheticism," "Red Feminism," and "The Rhetorical Construction of Gay and Lesbian Identity in Recent Nonfiction Film and Video"— to name a few. Overwhelmingly, these aim at what they call the de(con)struction of society and of America as we know it.

Naturally, the commissars in our government will finance their own projects. Others in government, as well as the larger corporations, pay "protection." Care to see what happens if your corporation refuses to hand over money to someone proposing to organize "group therapy for previously captive dolphins who now lead an alternative lifestyle"? Most would just as soon not find out.

Tax dollars flow to where they are most likely to effect the transformation of America into a Franco-Germanic–type society, where they guarantee the most efficient curtailment of freedom. Among the ancillary subsidies is legal assistance, bankrolled under cover of the Legal Services Corporation and similar fronts. These open the deep pocket of government and assist all persons of "good" standing to attack "evil" America. They are complemented by courts that encourage a steady flow of "plaintiffs" to help themselves to the cash of corporations or of productive individuals. The results contribute to the growing sense of uncertainty and fear.

EDUCATION

Nowhere does the battle rage as fiercely as in education. Predictably, the transformation of structure and content in the university filtered down until it had engulfed the entire educational establishment. While every day lip service is paid to "the crisis," and "solutions" are debated everywhere, the true purpose of the commissar state is making excellent progress. That purpose is *Gleichschaltung*—switching to parity, eliminating differences. Given that education is a slow and painstaking process, customarily pulled along by those at the top, the "upside-down society" needs to eliminate the very concept of "top." To this end, gaining knowledge is no longer regarded as the purpose of going to school. To this end, competition, evaluation in the form of grades, and reward for excellence must be eliminated. If there is no competition, there will be less and less competence. (Note the common root of the two words.) And if there is no more competence, there will be no more American excellence.

There will be no American anything—the primary purpose of the *National Standards in United States History*. The elimination of a nation's true history, expertly practiced in the Soviet Union and the Third Reich, guarantees commissars an uncontested field as they bring up generations with blanks instead of history in their heads. Those blank areas can be filled with anything the commissars invent. There are no beacons of the past, no common orientation, no grid of references to contradict the propaganda. That is why America's founding documents have been removed from the classroom, that is why civics classes have disappeared along with George Washington's birthday. History is the national memory. No history—no national memory—no identity. And, now that written history has been successfully purged, President Clinton has announced the "celebration of oral history" for the year 2000. Presumably, assorted tales from the realm of folklore will take the place of painstaking scholarship.

Among the successful tools of disorientation are constantly changing labels. In Europe, unlike the United States, streets are almost always named for people. My generation remembers how the German authorities, a few days after they marched in, began changing the names of streets and squares. Then, as soon as the Russians took over, they assigned *their* preferences. Many a street had three different names within a couple of years. The changes served several purposes at once. One was to erase the past, another was to keep everyone off balance, the third was to remind people who was boss. The practice originated in France when, after the great revolution of 1789, the names of the months were changed and the calendar designations "B.C." and "A.D." thrown out—an example warmly embraced by the authors of *Standards*. But the French did not stop there. As Napoleon's armies swept into the cities of Europe, they did away with ancient street names altogether, and numbered all houses consecutively.

France has long outgrown these afflictions, but the concept has been adapted for America as part of the assault on it by Franco-Germanic political thought. The changes have occurred in different ways. Street names have been left alone, but we must refer to people, conditions, institutions, and things with labels other than what they are, or have traditionally been called. Ostensibly, doing so will avoid pain and discomfort, although it is not quite clear how calling the jungle "rain forest" accomplishes this commendable goal. Calling American Indians "Native Americans" may give a moment of satisfaction to a relatively small number of people, but it deliberately affronts hundreds of millions who were born here. Of course, anyone familiar with the techniques of social-justice advocates will know that nothing happens by accident. "Native American" was carefully chosen to make the rest of us feel as if we did not really belong.

Speech codes are everywhere—at school, in the workplace, in editorial offices. But we shall never have to worry about losing the First Amendment, at least on paper. It will be retained for those who burn the flag or refuse to recite the Pledge of Allegiance. As for the rest of us, we were deprived of free speech once the *vocabulary* became controlled, once branding and sensitivity training were meted out as punishment for saying what we thought.

LANGUAGE

The words we use make up our language. Our language is not merely tradition or habit. Our institutions are intimately connected with English words and concepts, and so is the American identity. The thoughts and phrases that bespeak what we are happen to be next to impossible to convey in any other language. When newcomers arrived on these shores, it was not only a matter of necessity, of survival, that they learn English. It was the primary, indispensable step toward understanding our laws, our institutions, and our way of life.

When advocates of social justice clamor for the widespread use of other languages, the ostensible rationale given—accommodation of newcomers—has precious little to do with the true deep-seated reasons. Language is a vital part of the general assault on the English-speaking world. That assault was first launched in books and pamphlets, then in two world wars, and on into the Cold War. Now that the battlefield has moved inside America, a "final solution" has been found. The philosophical descendants of those who forbade listening to English-language broadcasts are now in the position to break the hegemony of English altogether. Currently, any language other than English will do, and, indeed, a host of languages take the place of English in state school systems such as those of New York or California. Nonetheless, a very special place has been given to Spanish, the language at the heart of the bilingual movement.

Ostensibly, it is the sheer number of Spanish speakers among newcomers that makes it a duty of the "caring and compassionate" to accommodate their "needs." The truth is that Spanish is not a language of successful political institutions, because neither in Spain nor in any of its Latin American progenies have there been developments comparable to ours. Hispanics who have become devoted Americans point out that attitudes in Spanish-speaking countries are so different as to render American ones perplexing for the first generation. Keeping a growing number of voting Americans within the confines of Spanish will make certain that they continue to live in oblivion of our political system and the principles upon which it was built.

For many years, people flocked to America in order to live in freedom. Today's newcomers far more likely seek economic advantage. Precisely for this reason, the need for English, and all it entails, should be obvious. Economic benefits depend on the preservation of our legal and political institutions.

This is not to suggest that immigrants forget the songs, the poems, the lore of the "old country," nor that Americans have nothing to learn from others. Clubs and associations, entire communities to keep old traditions alive, have always existed in this country. And Americans have always been eager students of the world. But distinctions must be made. It is wonderful to learn music from Germany, but not statecraft. It is exhilarating to observe how Japan creates exquisite gardens on tiny plots of land, but not how it treats its prisoners of war. It is impressive to see the many uses Mexicans find for the century plant, but not the way they run political institutions.

IMMIGRATION

Those determined to transform America have embarked on an immigration policy that matches their efforts elsewhere. Our borders are no longer controlled, our unconditional welfare benefits provide a powerful magnet, and our expectations of newcomers have been eliminated. Well-meaning persons argue that America has always been a country of immigrants, and that newcomers traditionally have contributed much fresh blood, fresh ideas, fresh impetus. But the immigrants who made those contributions were expected to be free from disease, to be able and willing to fend for themselves, and to have every intention of becoming American as quickly as possible. And they entered in possession of legal documents, issued after thorough vetting. None of the above applies anymore. In 1957 I waited in Vienna for two years before being granted a visa, and was required to furnish a sponsor; today, people simply get on a plane. In 1963 my brother arrived from Switzerland without his chest X ray, and he was promptly quarantined on Staten Island; today, not even advanced AIDS sufferers are turned away, and tuberculosis, conquered at last in the 1970s, is back. In 1964 my knowledge about the American system of government was examined in detail; today, a younger immigration officer might depend entirely on a script to ask questions about it.

HUMAN RELATIONS

While French and German theorists wrote volume after volume contemplating and prescribing the manner in which humans ought to live and work in a large society, America demonstrated day by day that the impossible could be achieved. People who had not been able to get along or get ahead in the country of their birth came to America and lived in peace and tranquility with their former enemies, foreign and domestic; it was unique and the source of greatest wonder.

The current immigration policy is a clear threat to that tranquility, and by no means the only one. In place of "America—envy of the world," there is only an uneasy coexistence of groups divided along fault lines in which the pressure is mounting. Human relations of all kind have been steadily deteriorating since the wholesale onslaught in the 1960s of Franco-Germanic political theory.

Nowhere has the damage been greater than in race relations. By 1968 segregationists had taken their last stand. The great majority of Americans was ready to dismantle racial obstacles and to make individual opportunity available for all. It would be a slow process. The most gifted and most ambitious would be first to the post; integration of the majority would take more time. But the continued fanning of the flames was a meal ticket for civil rights leaders, and suited the purpose of America's detractors. Consequently, no effort, however honest and strenuous, was sufficient to absolve Americans with fair skin from being branded "racist" every day, every hour. There is now a veritable army of people, indeed an industry, doing little else than complaining about white racism and filing lawsuits against all and sundry. The media offer a permanent bully pulpit, and young people grow up under the bombardment of hate speech—for once using the word in the real sense. And all the while commissars are hard at work regulating and legislating every area of human interaction, sure to cause resentment, and leading to possibly irreversible breakdown.

The general breakdown in human relations has converted America from success-society to problem-society. Nowhere is this more noticeable, indeed more alarming, than in the confusion surrounding the role, the place, of women.

Doubts about the capacity of women to perform men's work were swept away by World War II and, courtesy largely of the Katherine Hepburn–Spencer Tracy team, women were encouraged and men reminded of the fact often and emphatically. Facilitated by automation in the household, the two-wage-earner family emerged and, along with it, another Soviet institution—the daycare center.

Many believe that both parents work because a single income cannot provide for a family's needs. Many overlook the phenomenal growth of those "needs" during the last decades. Where previously a refrigerator and a washer and dryer sufficed, now entire batteries of kitchen machines, individual computers for every member of the household, Jacuzzis, and $200 gym shoes have become standard. That is one reason why so many women are in the workforce at the expense of the functioning family. Another one is the demand of feminists—and society's acquiescence—that women be represented in every field of human endeavor. From the vantage point of social justice, nothing less will be accepted as "fair." Demagoguery has so confused the issue that women who are not the least bit feminist are disturbed by suggestions that men might do better in selected areas. No amount of historic evidence is accepted because, of course, "all history has been the oppression of the oppressed, and women were always oppressed." Back when, Lenin recognized the explosive potential of this reasoning and salivated at the prospect in several essays.

Forcing women—anyone—into occupations where they deliver less than optimum performance reduces the overall strength of America. Society will atrophy if people do things not because society needs them, not because they are well-suited to the task, but just because they want to do it. No society can afford that luxury for long—it will come back to haunt us. In our defense establishment, it already has.

DEFENSE

American identity exists only so long as there is an America. America exists only as long as it can defend itself. "Providing for the common defense" was among the few specific reasons enumerated in the Preamble to the Constitution of the United States. Today, our federal government is engaged in literally thousands of activities—from affirmative action to zoological terrorism—neither mandated nor authorized in the Constitution. An optimist might conclude that the Clinton administration happens to have no particular interest in the defense of the realm. A realist is tempted to consider the possibility of a deliberate, gradual weakening of America's ability to resist the march toward an ultimate victory of Franco-Germanic political theory—"social justice"—worldwide.

The current executive branch is manned largely by those who in the 1960s declared their revulsion for the military in general, and America's military in particular. Given the attention focused on President Clinton's well-documented attitude and his efforts to evade military service during his early years, a genuine change of heart on his part would have been communicated to the American people. But not only has such an epiphany been absent; the evidence points to his use of every opportunity to reduce America's preparedness.

The first signs surfaced within weeks of the 1993 inaugural. More significant than choosing the issue of homosexuals in the military as his first presidential act was the instant reduction sought in the size and quality of the United States navy. No single concept symbolizes liberty as readily as free passage on the high seas. Whereas Spain, France, Russia, Germany, and Japan used their naval power—whenever they possessed them—to close down the sea lanes, first British, then American vessels kept them open. How much longer? The constant downgrading of facilities and equipment has been complemented by recurring attacks on the navy's personnel. From Tailhook to Admiral Boorda and beyond, an incessant barrage has been unleashed to destroy the navy's morale.

Not that other services have been spared. In fact, several other devices have been combined to reduce the fighting ability of our armed forces. Among these is the use of the armed forces for so-called humanitarian missions. These involve locations and require duties that confuse soldiers and negate much of their training. Among these is the shift from "aggressive defense" to "love thy neighbor" (metaphorically and literally), facilitated by the introduction of women and thinly veiled homosexuality in the barracks. Inviting sexual contact of every kind inside the military compound, moreover, has interfered with discipline and produced internal tensions, as well as new areas of litigation. And competence in the armed forces is eroded when women are interspersed with men in situations that require maximum strength, stamina, physical tolerance, and speed.

Then there is the matter of defense against missiles—the most likely threat of the future. The nation's hands are tied by the Clinton administration's determination that America adhere to the 1972 ABM Treaty with the Soviet Union. Since the Soviet Union no longer exists, who is the CBS-sufferer insisting that we continue unilateral observation of an arrangement detrimental to U.S. interests?

The sorry state of our armed forces is illustrated by a series of six air force plane crashes—including a stealth fighter and a B-1 bomber—in just one week in 1997. It is complemented by vast quantities of money being turned over to the Russian military, by opening our entire military establishment to Russian inspection, by providing China with supercomputers and other military hardware, by signing and ratifying a catastrophic Chemical Weapons Treaty, and by countenancing the establishment of Chinese bridgeheads at both ends of the Panama Canal and at Long Beach, California.

Here is some food for thought for those who believe that conflicts will occur in the future as they have in the past. Throughout the twentieth century, the United States navy was able to guarantee freedom of the seas because three vital points—the Suez Canal, the Panama Canal, and the Cape of Good Hope—remained under the control of the free world. Now, for the first time in memory, it will be possible for a potential adversary to choke off all three points simultaneously.

COMPETENCE, WORK ETHIC

It was 7:45 AM in Traverse City, Michigan, January 1964. We awoke to an ice-cold house. The furnace had shut down during the night. Being new in the community, I called a number from the Yellow Pages and explained we had a baby in the house. At 7:58—I looked at my watch—a van pulled up. In about six minutes, the serviceman located the trouble. In another two, he got the necessary part from his van. By 8:15, the unmistakable sensation of warm air came through the vents.

Knowing what to do and having the requisite tools used to be as American as apple pie. So was the notion that one worked for a living, that one worked as a habit. It was understood by all who lived here, and expected from all who came here. It gave America the edge. But it, too, had to be eliminated.

In schools, children are sidetracked by inane tasks, such as "saving the planet" and "world peace," while at the same time they are barely able to read or write their own names. Substituting ridiculous fantasies in place of realistic requirements engenders a sense of futility. Unattainable goals are certain to breed inertia. But then unattainable goals is what the search for social justice—socialism, communism—is all about.

In the workplace, competence is discouraged by hiring and promotion based on racial and gender quotas. In entertainment, we see the repudiation of the work ethic, as illustrated by such movies as *Regarding Henry*, *Reality Bites*, and many sitcoms on television. But it is not only the work ethic; ethical and moral standards are under attack everywhere.

RELIGION

Morality and religion have been engulfed by the World of Affirmative Action. Expressing preference for one kind of behavior, or one kind of religion, over another has not only been declared discriminatory, bigoted, and downright "unfair," but also special privileges have been demanded, and granted, for everyone who can demonstrate "other"-ness in any area. Originally, "other"-ness denoted persons who were not White Anglo-Saxon Protestants. Gradually, anyone with fair skin, of European origin, and with positive sentiments toward Christian religions came to be lumped with them, and classified as the oppressor. Eventually, heterosexuality became a negative and, finally, even black skin was insufficient to qualify the bearer as "good" if the person consorted with any of the above. The treatment meted out to a Thomas Sowell, Alan Keyes, Ward Connerly, or Clarence Thomas reveals the bitter truth.

The result is a veritable caste system, and, once again, we cannot have it both ways. Freedom and caste systems exclude one another. Caste systems and common sense exclude one another. Is a man still an oppressor if he is homosexual? Or black? Is a white person still an oppressor if she is female? Is a person disadvantaged if his native tongue is Spanish? What if that person descended from Spanish nobility? Or if he is a Muslim? Obviously, arbitrary decisions need to be made about "good"-ness. And just as obviously, commissars are needed to make those decisions.

America's founders decided against a state religion, but they would be astonished to find that a nativity scene exhibited in the village square was viewed as "unconstitutional." They regarded their Christian religion as a given. People of all religions, moreover, have found a greater degree of tolerance by this particular Christian country than by any other society—religious or secular. So as "not to offend Islam," President of the United States George Bush had to eat his Thanksgiving meal during Desert Shield aboard a ship while visiting American troops, stationed in Saudi Arabi to provide a living shield.

Eliminating ethics and morality—Christianity in whatever its manifestations—is vital to the "cause." Beginning with Descartes and Kant, a long line of French and German thinkers have pursued this course. And, as in every other realm, they have been successful. There is much unease, even among conservative Republicans, about the "political dangers" posed by the "Christian Right." It is as if a society beset by plagues of smallpox, typhoid, and cholera were suddenly to panic because someone sneezed.

As law is the repository of our rights, religion is the repository of our morality. There is ample evidence that a healthy balance of rights and morality gave us a society of free citizens and abundance. The Constitution was written to guarantee that balance. Religion in America never had the means to claim supremacy over the law. The danger today comes from the opposite end. Only the blind, and advocates of "social justice," fail to see the dangerous imbalance created by the proliferation of "rights" unrestrained by morality.

TRADITION, ALLEGIANCE, SOVEREIGNTY

"Toward Tradition" is the name of a Jewish organization which has found that "Jews are better off in a Christian than in a secular America." Yet during the past decades, many Jewish voices have joined with those who are committed to eliminating tradition. Next to the Old Testament, respect for tradition is the most visible Jewish contribution. Why this contradiction?

Another, not uncommon, contradiction surfaced in a recent federal court case, *Tisha Byars versus City of Waterbury Board of Education*. Miss Byars is a seventeen-year-old black girl who refuses to stand up during the Pledge of Allegiance—a habit she has engaged in since early childhood, as instructed by her father. The judge sees it as a case of exercising her First Amendment right, but that is not the point here. Miss Byars sued because the school—presumably as a result of her blanket rejection of America—did not qualify her for entering the National Honor Society. How does Mr. Byars explain to his daughter that it is all right to benefit from everything America offers, while demonstratively rejecting the symbols of its traditions? Another case of Compartmentalized Brain Syndrome.

Along with the Pledge of Allegiance, we honor a number of long-standing symbols of American identity. Among these are the flag and the national anthem. The flag has been subject to abuse since the 1960s. And our national anthem—as currently performed at sporting events, and various celebrations—is beginning to sound like some primordial chant. Troubling as are these assaults by private individuals, the real assault on America's identity occurs at the leadership level.

American identity finds its expression on the international stage as American sovereignty. American sovereignty, in fact, is the oldest constituent of our national identity—it goes all the way back to July 4, 1776. Watching the construction of "the bridge to the twenty-first century," there is every reason to fear that our sovereignty will have been thrown over the railing by the time we cross. The highly injurious Chemical Weapons Treaty was but a first step. The next one occurred in Kyoto late in 1997, where Vice President Al Gore signed off on crippling restrictions upon American industry, calling for significant reductions in American living standards in the name of "global warming." Apparently, it is solely emissions from America which are at fault, since other nations will be exempt. Or is it just another example of affirmative action? America has done better than most—it should now be slowed down until others catch up. In any event, the symbolism of Kyoto should not be lost on us. Half-a-century after hundreds of thousands of Americans died putting an end to Japan's aggression, and following decades of Japanese efforts to cripple America's car and electronics industries, it was in Japan that America surrendered its industrial leadership.

Symbolism, too, may be detected in the recent announcement by Jane Fonda's current husband (Ted Turner) that he would donate $1 billion for unspecified activities of the United Nations. The United Nations has been the main theater of our vanishing sovereignty for some time. In order to survive, the UN seeks jurisdiction in a number of new areas. Among these is the right to levy taxes, the placement of American military units under UN command, and the control of land masses under various environmental pretexts. The United Nation's primary target has always been the United States, the immense wealth and global position of our country being an incomparable asset. The accessibility of the Clinton administration offers a major opportunity for an expanded role, and slowly but surely the UN is making headway.

HYPOCRISY

On August 1, 1996, an agitated President Clinton confronted the White House Press Corps. "I don't believe that we should give special preferences to one group of people over others," he protested, "Do you? Do you?!" The outburst concerned the payment of

"Travelgate"-related legal expenses. But what about the raging national debate on preferences and quotas? Is that not about "special preferences"? Apparently not. Mr. Clinton went on to support affirmative action; the press corps was silent.

For lifelong observers, the mind-boggling hypocrisy of the Franco-Germanic side comes as no surprise. I recall one lone member of the communist establishment who refused the villa, the limousine, and use of the hidden, well-stocked food store at a time when the rest of the people lacked the bare necessities. He rode his bicycle to work and ate with the workers. His name was László Rajk, and they hanged him on a pretext.

Social-justice advocates typically demand behavior from others while exempting themselves. The majority of environmentalists would never dream of doing without the conveniences offered by modern technology.

For those who still believe that the protected status of "minorities" reflects genuine concerns for fair treatment, a look at Miami and southeast Florida might cause a rude awakening. The white, "Anglo" population is down to a mere 17 percent. There are vast areas where business is conducted exclusively in Spanish. Yet it is the Hispanics who enjoy "minority" status, while Anglos continue to bear the burden of the "oppressor."

Other examples of hypocrisy come in the form of "heads we win, tails you lose" scenarios. The recent celebrated case of an employee of Miller Brewing Company, who "offended" another employee by repeating a gag from the television show "Seinfeld," landed the employer in a situation in which the only question was which of the two employees would sue for damages. The "offended" if the "offender" were not fired, or the offender if he were. Similarly, the quandary with AIDS. Failure to express sufficient interest or compassion brands one a "homophobe." At the same time, suggesting that AIDS is especially rampant among homosexuals makes one a "bigot."

And how do we reconcile the insistence on women's equality with the insistence on cultural parity, when in most non-Western cultures women are clearly unequal?

But the ultimate hypocrisy is practiced by those who brand jokes as "ethnic slurs," and comments about a pretty woman as "harassment." These same people throw around slurs such as "homophobe," "racist," or "sexist" not only to harass, but to threaten the livelihood and the physical freedom of their fellow citizens. Then, adding insult to injury, they ask, "Why do you feel threatened?"

Unlike the aspiration for equality before the law, where our story began, the commissars of "social justice" demand conformity in our most private thoughts, our innermost sentiments. Conformity—not only to their failed theories, but to their every whim.

That, indeed, *is* threatening. It threatens to destroy the most successful society of all time.

IN CLOSING

CONCLUSIONS

THE LAST THREE decades have produced a debate about the very nature, the very existence of this nation. Unlike all previous political discourse, the question is a fundamental one: Is this country to remain the United States of America, pursuing the course of success as charted by America's founders, or are the people ready to accept an entirely different type of society—based on alien ideas with a record of catastrophic failure?

Use of the word "alien" should not be construed as a protectionist posture. Rather, it points to the deeply held conviction—evolved over decades—that the traditional debate between Left and Right, Democrat and Republican, even liberal and conservative, circumvents the fundamental question because the proposed alternative to "America-as-we-know-it" is of alien origin.

No more than four countries have ever engaged in a systematic examination of the manner and organization in which people live and work together successfully: Britain, France, Germany, and America. Individuals of other lands have made contributions of immense value, but these merged with the ongoing schools of political thought. The sequence in which the four primary schools

251

entered the field is also instructive. England, by creating the Magna Carta in 1215, preceded all others by several centuries. France's initial contribution was the work of Descartes during the seventeenth century. German thinkers and America's founders both joined during the eighteenth century.

One last time, a reminder that the present discussion is about political philosophy and its consequences, and that the conclusions drawn have no bearing on the arts, the sciences, or on people. The contributions of all four countries, in every field of endeavor, represent the highest plateau of human accomplishment. Indeed, the world would be much the poorer if it had to do without any one of them.

From the earliest beginnings, however, fundamental differences could be observed between English and French concepts of liberty, equality, and government. Those differences deepened as English thought became infused with, and enriched by, the Scottish Enlightenment, as well as by the contributions of the phenomenally inspired group of men we call the founders of America. Simultaneously, French thought might have been consumed in the flames of the French Revolution of 1789 and its aftermath, had it not been taken up by a most ambitious line of thinkers in Germany.

And so, we speak of a "Franco-Germanic" side, and an "Anglo-American" side, risking accusations of ethnic stereotyping where none is intended. Why the insistence on designation? Because disregard of the true origins of political ideas and agendas will stand in the way of their proper evaluation. Because ignorance of the origins of an idea, as well as the rationale behind it, allows advocates of that idea to hide its history, and to dress it in the attire of their choice. Honest discussions are hampered by the mistaken assumption that communism is Russian, or that communism and national socialism—nazism—are on opposite sides. Honest discussion is also hampered by camouflaging Franco-Germanic doctrine with traits that come naturally to Americans, such as caring and compassion.

Expositions and commentaries on both sides fill libraries. Yet at their simplest, the Franco-Germanic philosophical position may be characterized as attributing to human reason an unlimited capacity to comprehend, evaluate, and arrange the affairs of our world. Pursuant to this, the proper sequence in charting the future course for humanity calls for the theory to be developed first, and for people and events to conform to it. By contrast, the Anglo-American position regards human reason as bounded by limitations, and in need of moral guidance as it attempts to provide for the future. In this way of thinking, it is observation, experience, and lessons learned that form the basis of society's choice in organizing its institutions.

These contrasting positions determine respective approaches to all critical areas. In law, Franco-Germanic justice relies on a body of codes that are brought to bear on all subsequent disputes, verdicts to be delivered by professional jurists. In other words, theory first—practice to conform. Anglo-American common law builds a continually evolving library of case histories through which the combined experience of centuries offers guidance. Verdicts, handed down by lay jurors, reflect society's common sense of justice.

In economics, the Franco-Germanic side imposes theoretical "ideals" of production and distribution on all who participate. Failures must await revision of the theory before corrections in practice can take effect. Economic activity is thus regulated entirely by nonparticipants. The other, Anglo-American, side endeavors to secure conditions which will place the fewest obstacles in the path of individual creativity, and defers to the natural regulatory capacity of free competition. Accordingly, activity is determined by the participants, and protected by contract.

If human reason governs supreme, religion and morality have no place and no legitimate function, and indeed, such is the Franco-Germanic position. Right and wrong become arbitrary categories, "subject to change without notice." The same applies to values and, ultimately, to facts. Truth cannot survive in this scenario. Consequently, telling the truth is no longer a requirement, and taking an oath carries no meaning. Anglo-American thought recognizes the capacity of human reason to argue and advocate either side of an issue with equal success. Human reason, therefore, cannot be left solely to its own devices. Moral guidance is essential in reaching decisions that successfully walk the tightrope between the self-interest of an individual, and the community interest of society.

No area of human activity, no form of human interchange is unaffected by these fundamental differences. Since political thought functions as a foundation under, and as an umbrella over, all theaters of human activity, it reflects those same differences. To date, all applicable political thought has been the product of one or the other. A third possibility has yet to be articulated. Accordingly, on one side we find the perfect political theory and corresponding prescriptions which, it is claimed, will necessarily lead to the perfect society. In that perfect society, all will achieve perfect contentment. No evidence as yet exists to prove the upside potential of this Franco-Germanic doctrine, but the Soviet Union, Germany's Third Reich, and China's "Cultural Revolution" have demonstrated the downside. By contrast, Anglo-American thinkers have settled for limited, but attainable goals. One of these was to extend the blessings of liberty to more people than was possible in other forms of society. Liberty, in turn, produced an unprecedented accumulation of wealth, and increased access to it by a constantly growing number of people. We have seen the upside—it is called the United States of America.

Current political parlance refers to the two sides in a variety of ways. Of the first, "utopian," "statist," "collectivist," are the tamer labels, "totalitarian" and "socialist" the more aggressive ones. "Big government" is often used to skirt proper identification altogether. For the sake of clarity, I have settled on three different designations. "Franco-Germanic" refers to the origins, "the search for social justice" to the method, and "communism" to the end state. Renewed confirmation of the end state comes from no less an authority than Jiang Zemin, president of the People's Republic of China and head of China's Communist Party. On September 12, 1997, using words identical to the ones I first encountered in 1949, he identified socialism as a transitory phase, and communism as the goal.

The other side is often called "capitalism" which, as discussed earlier, is a deliberate misnomer for what is really free enterprise. This side is of Anglo-American origin, employs the rule of law as its method, and—although it acknowledges a number of aspirations and guiding principles—does not presume the existence of an end state.

If indeed only two major schools of political thought can be perceived, it stands to reason that they have taken consistently contrary positions. It is equally reasonable to assume that all major conflicts, though colored by additional participants and causes, have been clashes of the two sides. Both world wars, as well as the Cold War, fall in this category, as does the current debate about America's future.

Before the 1960s the United States was a participant only to the extent that it came to Britain's aid when necessary and, increasingly, assumed the position of chief defender of Anglo-American principles. As for the debate itself, America chose its path at the time of its founding, rendering moot any further discussion of the fundamentals. There remained only questions of improved implementation, and that process provided political parties with plenty of ground on which to disagree. Franco-Germanic ideas have been propagated by progressives, New Dealers, and socialists, not to mention outright communists. Yes, the graduated income tax and Social Security put dents into traditional concepts of self-sufficiency. But until recently no assault had been waged on America as a nation, on America as a concept, on the fundamental tenets of Anglo-American political thought. The 1960s unleashed all three.

The 1960s unleashed all three, but carefully avoided identifying the chief protagonist. There was the yearning for "love and peace." There was the resistance to a "horrible and unfair" war. There was an overdue Civil Rights Movement, and there was an equally "overdue" sexual revolution. All these, the nation was led to believe, were consistent with traditional American aspirations. All these, the reasoning went, were consistent with traditional debates about the implementation of American principles. The impatience of youth and the delay in the desegregation of black Americans may have produced an explosive mix, commentators mused, but different generations tend to be, well, different.

But if so, why the substitution of a "search for social justice" where once the law ruled? Why the proliferation of group privilege to the detriment of individual rights? Why the abolition of guaranteed property through regulation, redistribution, and entitlements? Why the daily assaults on our common American identity by hyphenation, bilingual ballots, multiculturalism, and phony history books?

Why? Because the overwhelming success of Anglo-American principles in society seemed to match the apparent Anglo-American invincibility on the field of battle. America was the "immovable object" standing in the way of the "irresistible force" Franco-Germanic ideology must prove itself to be. Dislodging the immovable object necessitated that Americans participate in significant numbers. That, in turn, would be possible only if:

(1) Americans were reminded frequently of their failures, and of various "wrongs" they and their country had inflicted on an ever-growing multitude

(2) Americans were persuaded that all apparently new ideas were, in fact, old American ideas and that by acting in accordance with those, they would become "better Americans"

(3) a constantly expanding range of people who had been "unfairly treated" and "deserving of special treatment" could be produced to keep the conscience of Americans troubled.

All three have come to pass. As a result, any suggestion that harm to America could be intended was made to sound preposterous. How can a "more perfect" implementation of "American ideals" possibly harm America?

The success of this campaign of deception is the compelling reason for hammering away at the *non-American* origin of the other side, and for placing the current debate about America's future in the context of centuries. Equally important is that we discover the connections that link hundreds or thousands of seemingly unconnected projects, campaigns, incidents, organizations, agendas, and publications that, together, constitute the all out effort to transform America from top to bottom.

The evidence confirms that the debate about America's future is not between divergent views of the same American principles, but pits political thinking and practice as developed mostly in France and Germany against the aspirations, principles, and institutions which have enabled this nation to succeed since the time of its founding.

Franco-Germanic and Anglo-American political thought are as different as night and day. Most people would prefer not to take note of this because Americans have a genuine aversion to finger-pointing and the "them-and-us" attitude. Most people would prefer not to take sides because Americans have a long tradition of staying close to the center. But, because the two sides are as different as night and day, there is, in reality, no "center" in the present scenario. There is only the Twilight Zone. Right now, that zone is crowded with people who prefer to describe themselves as "moderate," as "economic conservatives and social liberals," or something equally unrealistic.

Amidst all the bad news that pervades the preceding chapters, there is good news as well, once we clarify the origin and nature of the protagonists. The good news is that choosing the American side has no bearing on a person's traditional political preferences. There has always been, there must always be ample room for the resulting differences in the body politic. A healthy, dynamic society is hardly conceivable without them. And falling into the trap of Franco-Germanic ideas has not been an exclusive affliction of Democrats or liberals.

Better still, unlike other epidemics, this one may be arrested simply by a return to founding principles.

The recipe is not that we restore conditions as they existed in 1776, but that we resume living by the rule of law (as opposed to the rule of lawmakers); by observing the rights presumed and affirmed in the Constitution (as opposed to group privilege); by respect for property and contract (as opposed to forcible redistribution); and by reclaiming our common American identity (as opposed to emphasizing diversity).

Many will say that it has taken sixty or so years to get this far away from our founding principles; we cannot expect to reverse that overnight. The answer is that we may not have sixty years. The answer is that at the very least we must begin an open debate about fundamentals without further delay.

Many will say that we are in the midst of an unprecedented economic boom and ask why all this doomsday rhetoric? The answer is that our foundations are being eroded every day. Ever larger clouds loom over our ability to live, work, and act together as a nation, over our defense capability; it will be only a matter of time before our economy follows suit. An optimistic assessment of the future is supportable only if we undertake a realistic assessment of the present.

America's capacity, America's reserves are huge. We can continue downhill some way before the slide accelerates beyond recall. But President Jiang's constant reference to "socialism with Chinese characteristics"—meaning that the ideology is adapted to local conditions and requirements—seems to add substance to the proposition that we are witnessing the emergence of socialism with American characteristics.

The journey away from our American foundations toward that "other zone" began to accelerate some time around 1968. During the eight years of Ronald Reagan in the White House, the speed slowed considerably, but the direction of travel did not change. The early days of the 104th Congress held out the hope of traveling a few yards in the opposite direction. But today, we are again moving rapidly away from the "American zone."

As yet, our hands are on the controls. The tools are there, we still retain our national memory, and tens of millions remain in possession of their common sense. But some say the time has come to throw away the tools, to erase the memory, to ignore our common sense.

Should we?

As always, Americans will make a wise decision. The facts laid out here intend no more than to aid in that process.

A GLOSSARY OF TERMS
FREQUENTLY USED
(AND SOMETIMES MISUNDERSTOOD)

AFFIRMATIVE ACTION is a global approach that seeks to compensate for the variations in people's ability, industry, and fortune. It does not recognize differences among people as legitimate, maintaining that a lesser outcome can only result from discrimination or other forms of oppression.

BALANCE SHEETS are understood here as the known record of a person or a society's (group's) accomplishments and failures, as well as demonstrated positive and negative qualities. In the case of societies, contributions to mankind and harm inflicted on other societies are important aspects of the historic balance sheet.

BRANDING is the weapon used by advocates of social justice in place of reasoned argument in order to silence anyone who disagrees with their point of view. Certain "brandings" are staple (racist, sexist, extremist, homophobe), others are devised—and disseminated with impressive speed—to stifle specific political initiatives (tax-breaks for the wealthy, tax scheme, mean-spirited, uncaring).

CAPITALISM is a Marxist label for societies where the economic basis is free enterprise. Since free enterprise is not the realization of a theoretical model, it is not an "-ism." Because all advocates of Franco-Germanic political thought are engaged in some kind of -ism (socialism, communism, fascism, national socialism, etc.), an -ism to oppose became necessary.

COMMISSAR is a person whose activities stem from the disapproval of an existing society, and are directed to transform that society. Typically, a commissar dispenses benefits (often the taxpayers' money) to politically suitable recipients, or uses executive power and the court system to discipline, and inflict punishment upon, persons whose thinking or behavior deviates from prescribed norms.

COMPARTMENTALIZED BRAIN SYNDROME (CBS) is present when traffic between various areas of the brain is blocked and the sufferer is unable to connect bits of information. Such a person will not comprehend the cause-and-effect relationship between, for example, the abandonment of grading and falling standards of scholarship.

CONSPIRACY is often confused with a planned and focused **political campaign**. A small group meeting in secret to develop plans for a clandestine operation is a conspiracy. Working toward global political change is not. Because "conspiracy" is often invoked as a word of dismissal when we have no ready explanation for certain phenomena, caution is urged with respect to using the word loosely.

FAIRNESS means the consideration of the interest of both sides in a given situation—an attitude that seemed to come naturally to the English. No other language has even attempted a translation of the word. The English original is employed whenever the concept is cited.

MULTICULTURALISM supposedly means that American, French, German, British, Russian, Spanish, Dutch, Italian, Swiss, Austrian, Polish, Swedish, Czech, Hungarian, and Greek cultures are all the same, and that in order to achieve variety, they must be mixed with, or replaced by, the cultural products of Africa, Asia, and Latin America. In reality, multiculturalism is the application of affirmative action to cultures by eliminating considerations of greatness and intrinsic value.

POST-JUDICE is an opinion held or judgment made and applied to persons, societies, products, or situations based on individual and collective observance of past events—in other words, *after* the fact. It is often branded as "prejudice," which really means opinions held and judgments made *before* the fact.

SOCIALIST, by now, is a generic term. There have been so many versions of the original concept that a blanket definition can be neither precise nor exhaustive. All variants, however, agree on a restriction of individual freedom, a strong central authority, the usurpation of legislative and judicial prerogative by the executive branch of the government, and some suspension of property rights. The following are the best-known variants.

> BOLSHEVIK means "majority," which Lenin declared his faction to be as soon as it was defeated by the genuine majority, whom Lenin thereafter called "Menshevik," or "minority." Officially named "The Soviet Union's Communist (Bolshevik) Party," Lenin's organization was inherited by Stalin, and was probably responsible for more suffering and deaths than any other.

> COMMUNIST customarily describes members of various Communist parties—persons who labored toward

the ultimate arrival of communism and saw it destined to secure the best future for mankind. With the decline in both the membership and the importance of Communist parties, the label today is more appropriate to persons who hold that the aggressive pursuit of "social justice" is the path to follow.

FASCIST refers to a member of an Italian political party, founded and led by Benito Mussolini, who was expelled from the Socialist Party of Italy and went on to start his own. The structure was a copy, the concept a variant of other socialist parties. "Fasces," a bundle of twigs with an ax, were carried before consuls of ancient Rome. Mussolini adopted the symbol, hence the name "fascist."

NAZI was a nickname given to members of the National Socialist German Workers' Party, Hitler's outfit, which formed the core of the Third Reich. Yet another variation on the theme of socialism, national socialists acquired their nickname through a cartoon character, "Ignaz," nicknamed "Nazi," who was the stereotypical Jew. Before the horror of reality set in, it seemed a good joke on the posturing, parading, clearly antisemitic national socialists to share a nickname with a Jewish cartoon character. Later, Stalin thought up the switch of applying the Italian "fascist" designation to German national socialists in order to erase from memory that the nazis were, in fact, socialists.

Note: In Hungary alone, the communist party went through four complete name changes during its tenure. It is an integral part of socialist operational methodology to make an instant switch once a label has been tainted with "mistakes" (such as too many atrocities), or when a new compendium of deceptions is about to be announced.

SOCIAL JUSTICE is the term used to make its proponent appear to be a person who truly cares about the fate of others. As opposed to those who help actual, visible, flesh-and-blood individuals in need, champions of social justice speak in broad generalities, and advocate the redistribution of assets, means, and opportunity to "the disenfranchised," the "underprivileged," and others in the abstract. Typical is the absence of specific, or even consistent, goals beyond the requirement of making incessant demands in order to justify the confiscation of other people's property.

COMMISSAR BIOGRAPHIES

IN THE FALL of 1954, the Central Committee of the Communist Party sent a new secretary to Budapest's famed Liszt Academy of Music to head the Academy's party organization. The new man thought it appropriate to present himself to the nation's senior musician, Zoltán Kodály. He knocked on the door of the master's studio, went inside, and explained the reasons for his visit.

Kodály, as was his habit, looked out the window for some time. He then asked, "What happened to your predecessor?"

"He went back to his trade."

"What was his trade?"

"He is a hatmaker."

"And what is your trade?"

It was now the secretary's turn to consider.

"I've always worked in the movement."

Kodály turned around from the window and regarded his visitor for the first time. Then he looked out the window once more and asked,

"To what will *you* go back?"

The 1960s gave birth to a new type of American: the professional political activist, whose entire working life would be spent in "the movement." The illustrations reveal a remarkable similarity in these lives, the two most obvious being the absence of participation in an enterprise, trade, or profession—in any nonpolitical occupation—and the use of tax revenues as the source of income.

To draw attention to a pattern, rather than to specific individuals, the names and current offices held appear at the end of each *curriculum vitae* in brackets.

The following information was obtained either from the appropriate government department, or copied off the Internet. In each case, the information is available to the public.

IKP was a Deputy Assistant Attorney General in the Civil Rights Division of the U.S. Department of Justice from June 1994 until January 1997, when she assumed her current position. As a Deputy Assistant Attorney General she directed the work of the division in the enforcement of federal civil rights laws in the areas of employment and education. Ms. P. was also responsible for major activities in the area of affirmative action, in particular the supervision of litigation in defense of federal affirmative action programs and of the work of the Division in the government-wide review of federal affirmative action programs.

Assistant Secretary NVC is responsible for enforcing the Federal civil rights statutes that protect the rights of students to an equal educational opportunity without regard to race, color, national origin, sex, disability, or age. The civil rights laws extend to a wide range of educational institutions that receive Federal funds. These include nearly every school district and college and university in the country as well as proprietary schools, libraries, museums, and correctional facilities.

C. considers discrimination of any form to be a serious barrier to equal access and to the achievement of educational excellence in this country by all students. She believes effective civil rights

Prior to joining the division, Ms. P. was for fifteen years the director of the Women's Rights Project of the American Civil Liberties Union. In that capacity she became a nationally recognized expert in sex discrimination and civil rights law and practice. She conceived, designed, supervised, and participated in major ground- breaking litigation and major *amicus curiae* briefs under the Constitution and civil rights laws on discrimination issues in employment, education, public accommodations (including insurance), health care, and the military. She has written and spoken extensively on these subjects. She was responsible for the coordination of the ACLU's activities in the field of women's rights, for leading the development of the project's policies and programs, and for fund raising.

Prior to joining the ACLU staff, Ms. P. served as deputy director of the National Employment Law Project (a Legal Services support center), and as a staff attorney with the Law Reform Unit of the Legal Aid Society of Cleveland.

enforcement can help all persons in making the most of their individual capacities and talents. As the head of the Department's Office for Civil Rights, C. seeks to establish a civil rights compliance program directed at affording all students the opportunity to realize their educational potential from the moment they enter the classroom.

The assistant secretary is a distinguished litigator, with a long record of advocacy in the areas of educational equity and school finance reform. From 1985 until joining the department, C. was the regional counsel for the Mexican American Legal Defense and Education Fund (MALDEF), based in San Antonio, Texas. From 1983 to 1992 she also served as national director of the MALDEF Education Litigation and Advocacy Project, acting as lead counsel in a number of education-related lawsuits.

C. was a public school teacher in 1974 and again in 1979. In addition, she has been active with many San Antonio community organizations including the Center for Hispanic Health Policy Development, the Texas

A native New Yorker, Ms. P. received her A.B. degree in history from Goucher college in 1967 and graduated from the Boston University School of Law in 1970.

(*Isabelle Katz Pinzler, Acting Assistant Attorney General for Civil Rights, U.S. Dept. Of Justice*)

Human Rights Commission, and the City of San Antonio Health Facilities Commission. She has received a number of awards, including the Public Policy Recognition (San Antonio) and special citations from the Hispanic Chamber of Commerce and *Hispanic Business* magazine's 100 Influentials.

C. graduated summa cum laude with a B.S. from Pan American University in 1973, and from Harvard Law School (at age twenty-two) in 1977.

(*Norma V. Cantú, Ass't Secretary, U.S. Department of Education, Office of Civil Rights*)

JAW was sworn in as General Counsel to the U.S. Department of Education on June 28, 1993. She manages a staff of more than eighty attorneys providing legal services to the department. (W. assumed the title of Acting Under Secretary of Education in July 1996.)

The Office of General Counsel interprets laws affecting department operations, drafts and reviews regulations and legislation, represents the

BLL is one of the country's leading civil rights attorneys, with a long and distinguished history of defending the rights of all Americans. Mr. L. has spent his twenty-three–year legal career seeking equal opportunity for all people and working diligently against discrimination in all forms, including in employment, housing, voting, and education. Mr. L. has extensive experience in many areas of civil rights law, including employment discrimination, access to department in litigation, and advises the secretary on policy issues. The office also manages the department's ethics and regulations programs.

Previously, W. was an associate professor of law at American University in Washington, D.C., where she taught civil procedure and civil rights. She also worked as a lawyer on a variety of civil rights, race, and gender equity issues, and was deputy director for public policy at the Women's Legal Defense Fund in Washington.

Formerly, she was the deputy director of the Lawyers' Committee for Civil Rights Under Law and assistant general counsel for educational equity at the U.S. Department of Education. She was executive assistant and legal counsel to the chair of the Equal Employment Opportunity Commission and special assistant to the director of the Office for Civil Rights in the former U.S. Department of Health, Education and Welfare.

W. has served on numerous boards and committees and has health care, prevention of lead poisoning in poor children, access to public transportation, and equal access to education.

Known as a skilled consensus builder, Mr. L. is an excellent litigator who has always fought zealously for his clients and who has also known how and when to bring a case to close through effective, pragmatic settlements that serve the interest of all parties. His honest, reasoned approach has won the respect of opponents and colleagues alike.

Before his appointment at the Department of Justice, Mr. L. lived in Los Angeles and served as Western Regional Counsel for the NAACP Legal Defense and Education Fund (LDF), the civil rights law firm founded by the late Supreme Court Justice Thurgood Marshall. Mr. L. began his legal career at LDF in New York as associate counsel in 1974. In 1983 he joined the Center for Law in the Public Interest, a noted public interest law firm in California, and served for five years as supervising attorney for Civil Rights authored many articles on civil rights, employment discrimination, and women of color in the work place.

W. is a graduate of the Georgetown University Law Center and Howard University.

(Judith A. Winston, Executive Director, The President's Racial Advisory Board)

Litigation. In 1988 he rejoined LDF. Mr. L. also served as an adjunct professor of Political Science at Fordham University, and as counsel to the Asian American Legal Defense and Education Fund.

Mr. L. was born and raised in New York City, where his parents owned a small laundry. He credits his late father, who experienced bigotry despite his proud military service to his country, with providing the inspiration for a career in civil rights law. After graduating from the Bronx High School of Science, Mr. L. won a scholarship to Yale University, where he benefitted from an affirmative action program to include minority students. Through his hard work, Mr. L. graduated Phi Beta Kappa, *magna cum laude* in 1971. Mr. L. graduated from Columbia University Law School in 1974.

(Bill Lann Lee is Acting Assistant Attorney General for Civil Rights, U.S. Dept. of Justice.)

Note: In evaluating Mr. Lee's biography, it is important to realize that Yale University had no affirmative action program before 1973.

AN EXCERPT FROM "THE BATTLE FOR AMERICA'S SOUL"
(THE POTOMAC PAPERS, MARCH 1995)

PHILOSOPHICAL FOUNDATIONS

If, as I had suggested, Fascism, Nazism, Communism, Bolshevism are not really different in methods and outcome, if they are branches of the same tree, it stands to reason to look for shared roots. Conventional wisdom holds that Communism grew out of Karl Marx's writings, while it is customary to trace Nazism's origins mostly to Social Darwinism. Such oversimplifications are misleading. Yet, one might as well begin with Marx, since his name is associated both with the rise of Communism (the prophet to follow), and with the rise of Nazism (the devil to exorcize). The first question is, then, "Why Marx?"

During the second half of the nineteenth century, those who wished to be informed and enlightened, and those who looked for guidance in their endeavors to work toward a better future, were faced with an embarrassment of riches: By then, every facet of life and of the universe had been subjected to examination, analysis, and synthesis. Philosophers, contemplating past and present, concerned themselves with abstractions. Social theorists proposed practical changes to the tangible world in an effort to improve upon it. There

273

even were dreamers who described visions of a "Heaven on Earth" to arrive at some future date.

One, and one alone, presumed to present himself as all these things: philosopher, social theorist, dreamer, even scientist. In addition, he claimed the ability to foretell the "inevitable" future—thus engaging in prophesy as well. That one was Karl Marx. This last presumption elevated his doctrines from the crowded library of less-than-first-rate thinkers to the unique potential of a religion. And because German philosophy at the time was going in the direction opposite from religion (witness Nietzsche), it should not come as a surprise that Marx was originally adopted in Russia—the country where religion was indispensable and where only a new orthodoxy could replace the existing one. Not unexpectedly, opposition to Marx took on an equally religious fervor in the Third Reich.

Despite today's popular association of Communism with Russia or China, the philosophical underpinnings, then, appear to be German but not simply because Marx was born in Germany or because his closest collaborator was Friedrich Engels. The development of Marx's thought process was predicated on his studies of Hegel (Dialectics) and of Feuerbach (Materialism), to mention but two decisive German influences. While it is true that Marx's sudden burst of writing activity was occasioned by Proudhon, who was French, German thinkers by this time, owing to numbers as well as to weight, had begun to assume the place of primary importance in the realm of metaphysics and to eclipse the French when it came to the construction of philosophical systems. Kant, Hegel, Schopenhauer and (even if his counts as the "anti-system") Nietzsche are obvious examples, but intellectual giants like Lessing, Goethe, Schiller or Humboldt—who would not even be listed under "philosophy"—would easily qualify as well.

Nevertheless, the argument becomes troublesome at this point. While the predominance of German Classical Philosophy is obvious when one considers that even a Dane such as Kierkegaard is inseparable from his relationship to Hegel, it is equally true that Hegel is unthinkable without Plato. We might, then, use a currently-fashionable term and recognize in all this the "German reception of Plato." Even Social Darwinism seemed to owe its promulgation to a German—Ernst Haeckel—whose "reception" of Charles Darwin's Theory of Evolution resulted in its application to human societies. But on further investigation we find the fundamental thesis behind Social Darwinism already proposed in Plato's *Gorgias*. Socrates rejects it, but not convincingly. Does this make Plato responsible for Hitler and Stalin?

The initial answer has to be "No," and it applies to some extent even to Marx or Haeckel. Lenin sought to dispense with Marx as the theoretical foundation as soon as the revolution was on track. Hitler accepted Social Darwinism only so long as the "natural selection" went his way; when Nature failed to eliminate "inferior" races, the SS stepped in. If any, the specific responsibility of the thinker is in having provided a repertory of texts which can be turned into pretexts with little difficulty. There is, however, a more comprehensive responsibility in the whole notion of self-contained systems, with all their misleading implications.

The construction of philosophical systems which ask the questions and attempt to provide the answers to all aspects of the human condition proved eminently compatible with German intellectual temperament. To be sure, the Encyclopaedia Britannica speculates that Marx would have strongly disapproved of practices adopted by Communist parties in his name; how much more so Hegel or Plato. Similarly, there is no reason to assume that Haeckel or Nietzsche would have participated in the Nuremberg rallies of the Nazi Party. Yet, the proclivity of creating systems, the predisposition to search for and provide all-encompassing answers, the assumption that such answers even exist are, by the available evidence, characteristically German. These qualities have given the world the St. Matthew Passion, Faust, the Ninth Symphony. In the search for the "ideal world," however, these same qualities were employed to justify the termination of life for millions and the prescription of life for all others, be it in the Pan-German Empire, in the Soviet, even in the Chinese Empire.

Notwithstanding French socialists, syndicalists and (later) existentialists, the spotlight of history illuminates a long and distinguished line of German thinkers by the time we approach the end of the nineteenth century. They would have, no doubt, reigned sovereign over the landscape, and in the minds of those who eternally seek "improvements" in the organization of society, were it not for the alternative to metaphysics which came from but a single direction.

THE ALTERNATIVE APPROACH

Taking his cue, perhaps, from what began in 1215 at Runnymede, it was John Locke who, nearly five hundred years later, identified and settled for *attainable* goals. He and Adam Smith seem to have broken with the two-thousand-year-old search for what is *right*, and substituted an inquiry into that which was *possible*.

It would be consistent with the previous argument to suggest that the sober modesty of Locke and Smith was as much a reflection on the British temperament as Hegel or Nietzsche was on the German. To be sure, subsequent German philosophical systems are unthinkable without the French Descartes; profound insight into human nature was offered first by the Italian Machiavelli. I submit, however, that it was the fusion of Descartes' metaphysics with German intellectual attitudes, and the fusion of Machiavelli's political science with British patience which eventually produced such diametrically opposing views of the world. The "pedigree" could be pursued further by linking Thomas Hobbes' translation of Thucydides (the greatest of Greek historians) with Machiavelli (founder of the modern philosophy of history), and the resulting acceptance of human nature.

Be that as it may, we have Locke and Smith. The astonishing influence of their thought is comparable only to the success of the societies which paid attention to them. Without diminishing the significance of Locke's lasting pronouncements on the limited role of government, the separation of powers, the relationship of the individual to the community, or the full roster of civil liberties, one is tempted to say that his genius lay in the very acceptance of certain limitations, which is at the heart of his *Essay Concerning Human Understanding*. Free from what Friedrich Hayck calls the "fatal conceit," Locke presents his *chef d'oeuvre* fully cognizant of inconsistencies, perhaps to signal that these are forever inherent in the human condition. Critics continue to cite the "superficiality of his treatment." In fact, Locke is refreshingly different in that he neither implies that he is privy to divine insight nor finds himself in need of declaring God "dead" to make his point. English thinkers, unlike their German counterparts, did not seek to challenge religion—a most significant difference in approach and one which contributed in no small measure to the outcome.

Locke's discovery of freedom in voluntary obedience was further defined by Adam Smith who proposed that "every man, as long as he does not violate the laws of justice, is left perfectly free to pursue his own interest his own way." From Smith's "natural liberty" to Hayek's "extended order of human cooperation," the observer beholds the very opposite of those systems which seek to chart the course for humanity based on the speculative powers of "pure" reason. Locke's image of the world issued from a combination of sense-perception and reflection (others call it empiricism) and never required a leap of faith. In place of any formal social contract, which Locke himself already had held to be discredited, an implied contract emerged in time: It predicates the guarantee of liberty and of individual rights upon the concession by the individual of those same rights to every other individual in the community.

INDEX

279

static state, 57
statistics, 168, 183
Stewart, Jimmy, 7–8, 218

terminology, 165, 173
terrorism, 138
Third Reich, 7–8
tobacco, 180–181
Tocqueville, Alexis de, 202, 206
travel, 75
Truman Doctrine, 110
trust, 5
truth, 132
Turner, Ted, 245

UN, 245
uniforms, respect, 148

values, 25
Vazsonyi, Vilmos, 7
Vazsonyi, Balint, 4, 10
victims, 170
Vietnam, 19, 111–112, 115
vocabulary, 18, 234, 254
Voltaire, 94–95
volunteerism, 207

war, cultural, 15, 20
Washington, George, 49, 96,
    202, 207, 233
Watergate, 115
welfare system, 156
western civilization, 43
women: rights, 77, 80, 214, 217;
    men and, 161, 213–15, 238
work ethic, 156, 205, 207,
    241–242
World Bank, 199

World War I, 50, 107–109
World War II, 112, 238
Yalta conference, 9

Zaire, 44
Zemin, Jiang, 18